Jeff Bezos and Amazon

INTERNET BIOGRAPHIES™

Jeff Bezos and
Amazon

JENNIFER LANDAU

ROSEN
PUBLISHING®

New York

For my sisters, who never ever give up!

Published in 2013 by The Rosen Publishing Group, Inc.
29 East 21st Street, New York, NY 10010

First Edition

Library of Congress Cataloging-in-Publication Data

Landau, Jennifer, 1961–
Jeff Bezos and Amazon/Jennifer Landau.—1st ed.
      p. cm.—(Internet biographies)
Includes bibliographical references and index.
ISBN 978-1-4488-6914-5 (lib. bdg.)
1. Bezos, Jeffrey—Juvenile literature. 2. Amazon.com (Firm)—
History—Juvenile literature. 3. Booksellers and bookselling—
United States—Biography—Juvenile literature. 4. Businessmen—
United States—Biography—Juvenile literature. 5. Internet
bookstores—United States—History—Juvenile literature.
6. Electronic commerce—United States—History—Juvenile
literature. I. Title.
Z473.B47L36 2013
381'.4500202854678—dc23

                                          2011038405

Manufactured in the United States of America

CPSIA Compliance Information: Batch #S12YA: For further information, contact Rosen Publishing, New York, New York,
at 1-800-237-9932.

Contents

INTRODUCTION

In July 2011, the *New York Times* reported that profits for Amazon.com, the largest retailer in the world, fell by 8 percent in the second quarter of 2011. Yet in the same time period, revenue—the total amount of money coming in to the company—rose 51 percent, to $9.9 billion. Amazon explained the dip in profits by pointing to its continuing investment in technology and warehouses, including a 900,000-square-foot (83,612.7-square-meter) warehouse in Indiana.

As the *New York Times* put it, "The company is apparently selling so many things to so many people that it can make sizable investments and barely feel the pain." Jeff Bezos, Amazon's founder and chief executive, remarked in a statement at the time that "[l]ow prices, expanding selection, fast delivery and innovation are driving the fastest growth we've seen in over a decade."

Bezos has always emphasized growth over profit for Amazon. His willingness to take risks and delay profits in his constant quest for innovation are some of the qualities that have made him—and the company he built—such a phenomenal success.

Jeff Bezos holds Amazon's first sign while standing in the company's Seattle headquarters in 1995. The sign was quickly spray-painted before Bezos gave an interview about his company with a Japanese television station.

When Amazon began its online business in 1995, most people used the Internet for e-mail and little else. Bezos had done his homework, however, and knew that Web usage was growing at a rapid rate. He set out to build an online retailer so user-friendly that people who shopped there would soon become loyal customers.

Many customers did just that. By 2010, Amazon had total annual sales of $34.2 billion and an estimated thirty-three thousand employees worldwide. In 2011, Bezos's personal fortune was listed at more than $18.1 billion. He was ranked thirtieth on the *Forbes* list of world's billionaires, while Amazon was ranked seventh on CNNMoney's (http://money.cnn.com) list of most admired companies.

Bezos thrives on constantly adapting to the needs of the marketplace. Whether that means adding to the list of merchandise Amazon offers, expanding into new areas like self-publishing and designer fashions, or fine-tuning every aspect of how a warehouse operates, Bezos's goal is to make the experience as seamless as possible for every Amazon customer.

Bezos is also comfortable acknowledging the techno-logical and design brilliance of others, including the late

Steve Jobs. According to the *Los Angeles Times*, at the time of Jobs's death, Bezos praised the Apple cofounder and CEO. "Steve was a teacher to anyone paying attention," Bezos said in a statement. "[A]nd today is a very sad day for everyone who cares about innovation and high standards."

It is Bezos's zeal and tirelessness that has seen Amazon through the inevitable ups and downs that come with building a start-up that began in a garage into a worldwide powerhouse. Now in his late forties, Bezos has a happy home life, as well as wide-ranging interests and investments. Amazon remains the cornerstone of his work life, however, as Bezos is determined to keep his company at the forefront of technological and commercial innovation.

CHAPTER 1

Young Visionary

On the morning of November 13, 2006, a test spacecraft named *Goddard* was launched 285 feet (86.9 m) into the west Texas sky and then safely returned to the launch pad. The aerospace company responsible for this flight was Blue Origin, founded in 2000 by Jeff Bezos. Bezos is the founder of Amazon.com, which is listed on its Web site as "Earth's most customer-centric company."

According to Blue Origin's Web site, the goal of the company is "to lower the cost of spaceflight so that many people can afford to go and so that we humans can better continue exploring the solar system." What is the motto of Blue Origin? The Latin phrase *Gradatim Ferociter*, which translates roughly as "step by step, fiercely."

This motto could easily sum up the life and career of Jeff Bezos. With drive, optimism, and great faith in his ability to make his mark on the world, Bezos has transformed not only how people shop, but also how they interact with technology. From a young age, he has held tight to his dreams and his belief that well-planned, incremental steps are the best way to achieve long-lasting results.

According to Robert Spector's *Amazon.com: Get Big Fast*, Ursula "Uschi" Werner, Bezos's high school girlfriend, believed that Bezos founded Amazon so that he could eventually earn enough money to build a spaceship. Certainly, as a youth Bezos thought of becoming an astronaut. In his high school valedictory speech, he talked about how the colonization of space was a way to secure the future of the human race in our fragile world. Bezos was a *Star Trek* fan and truly believed in space as being the final frontier.

Whether Bezos viewed spaceflight as his ultimate goal is debatable. What is not debatable is that from an early age, Bezos has been on a path toward greatness. This path has been powered by his instinct for where the latest innovation would lead the United States and his determination to be at the forefront of that innovation.

A CLOSE-KNIT FAMILY

Jeff Bezos was born Jeffrey Preston Jorgensen in Albuquerque, New Mexico, on January 12, 1964. His mother, Jackie Gise Jorgensen, was a seventeen-year-old high school student when Jeff was born. Jackie and Jeff's father, Ted Jorgensen, split up soon after Jeff's birth, later divorcing. While working at a bank after community college, Jackie met Miguel "Mike" Bezos, and they married in 1968. Jackie and Mike went on to have two more children, Jeff's sister, Christina, born in 1970, and brother, Mark, born in 1971.

Mike adopted Jeff, who had no contact with his biological father. When Jeff was told of the adoption at age ten, it didn't disturb him. He later said that finding out that he needed glasses was more of a blow than discovering that Mike Bezos wasn't his biological father, as he considered Mike his dad. The only time Ted Jorgensen entered Jeff's mind was when he was filling out a form at the doctor's office and wondered about his medical history.

The Bezos family was a laid-back and happy one. Jeff had two loving parents, as well as a lot of contact with his maternal grandparents, who owned a ranch called the Lazy G in Cotulla, Texas. Jeff was particularly close with his maternal grandfather, Lawrence Preston Gise, known as "Pop." Pop had worked for the Atomic Energy Commission, a fact that might explain Bezos's later investment in General Fusion, a nuclear fusion company.

From an early age, Jeff showed that he had an inquisitive mind and a determined spirit. When he turned three, he wanted to graduate from a crib to a bed. His mother thought that he was too young for a bed, so Jeff took matters into his own hands, attempting to dismantle the crib with a screwdriver. At the Montessori preschool he attended, Jeff would often become so fascinated by a

Operation Pedro Pan

Mike Bezos was a supportive and loving father to young Jeff. Mike's own background, however, was far from easy. In 1962, fifteen-year-old Mike fled Cuba as part of Operation Pedro Pan (Peter Pan), which sent more than fourteen thousand children to the United States without their parents. The families of these children hoped their sons and daughters would have a chance at a better life in America than under Fidel Castro's Communist government. Mike didn't speak English when he arrived in Florida. He moved to a Catholic mission in Delaware, where he lived with fifteen other children.

Despite these difficulties, Mike finished high school and graduated from the University of Albuquerque thanks to a scholarship for refugees from Castro's Cuba. When Mike met and married Jackie Jorgensen, the two provided Jeff and his siblings with a safe and secure environment in which to thrive. Surely, Jeff's boundless optimism stems in part from having been raised by a man of great character who believed in his son every step of the way.

project that his teachers would have to lift up his chair and physically move him to the next activity. Throughout Jeff's boyhood, both of his parents encouraged his unique gifts. His mother would sometimes drive to RadioShack multiple times a day to get Jeff the parts he needed for his various inventions, which included booby traps and alarms.

THE LAZY G

From the ages of four through sixteen, Jeff spent three months of every year working on the Lazy G ranch with his grandfather, Pop. As an engineer for Exxon, Mike Bezos had to move his family often, beginning with a transfer from Albuquerque to Houston, Texas. Although Jeff didn't mind the frequent moves, summers at the Lazy G provided him with both consistency and challenge. Jeff loved spending time with Pop, and the work taught him to be resourceful and self-reliant, two traits that every successful entrepreneur must possess. He admired the "get it done" philosophy of ranchers and later admitted to having a bit of the cowboy in him.

On the ranch, Jeff helped his grandfather repair a D-6 Caterpillar bulldozer, even building cranes to help lift the gears out of the machine. He helped brand the cattle and learned how to meld metals as well. According to Gene Landrum's *Entrepreneurial Genius: The Power of Passion*, Jackie Gise Bezos believed that Jeff's time working at the

Lazy G taught him that there "really aren't any problems without solutions. Obstacles are only obstacles if you think they're obstacles. Otherwise, they're opportunities."

Jeff's grandfather, who had worked for the Department of Defense as well as the Atomic Energy Commission, nurtured Jeff's love of science. When Pop came to visit Jeff, he would bring amateur radio kits, and the two of them would build radios together. Like Jeff's parents, Pop had faith in the inquisitive boy who tore through science kits and dreamed of becoming an astronaut.

EARLY SUCCESS AT SCHOOL

Once in Houston, Texas, Jackie and Mike enrolled Jeff in a pilot program for gifted students at River Oaks Elementary School. Although attending the school required a 40-mile (64.4-kilometer) round-trip ride per day, Jeff stayed at the school for three years in order to keep his keen intellect engaged.

Jeff continued to work on science projects at home. These projects included building a hovercraft from a vacuum cleaner and an aluminum foil–covered umbrella that was part of an experiment in cooking with solar power. At River Oaks, Jeff was fascinated by an infinity cube, which was a cube lined with mirrors that used motors to make the mirrors move. When you placed an item inside the mirror-lined cube, you saw its reflection from an infinite number of shifting angles, making it seem as if you were staring into space. Jeff asked his mother to buy him an infinity cube, but she said that $20 was too much to pay for a toy. Jeff's solution was to gather the parts and make his own.

While at River Oaks Elementary, Jeff and a few classmates learned how to program an electromechanical typewriter called a Teletype machine that could be connected to a mainframe computer via a modem. Jeff's interest in and aptitude for technology was apparent at an early age.

HIGH SCHOOL STAR

When Exxon transferred Mike Bezos to Florida, Jeff enrolled at Palmetto High School in Miami. Jeff set his sights on becoming the top student in his class, which necessitated taking on extra projects and entering competitions. Jeff's honors included winning the school's Best Science Student award three years in a row, as well as the award for Best Math Student during his junior and senior years. His essay "The Effect of Zero Gravity on the Aging Rate of the Common Housefly" earned him a trip to NASA's Marshall Space Flight Center in Huntsville, Alabama, which surely thrilled a teenage boy so taken with spaceflight. True to his goal, in 1982 Jeff was named the valedictorian of his class of 680 students.

Schools

'New pathways of thought' on summer breeze

By SANDRA DIBBLE
Herald Staff Writer

Give them just two weeks, the two Palmetto High graduates say — just two weeks — and they could "open new pathways of thought" for some fifth-grade pupils.

Ursula Werner and Jeff Bezos, Palmetto classes of 1981 and 1982 respectively, are conducting a 10-day course this summer for 10-year-old students, teaching them about Jonathan Swift's book *Gulliver's Travels*, about black holes in outer space, about electric currents and nuclear arms limitations talks, about how to operate a camera.

They call it The Dream Institute.

"We don't just teach them something," said Bezos. "We ask them to apply it."

Between 9 and 12 every weekday morning since June 21, Bezos' comfortable, carpeted bedroom becomes a classroom for Christina, Mark, Howard, Merrell and James.

If the course and setting are unusual, so are the teachers. Werner and Bezos were valedictorians at Palmetto. Both have won Silver Knight awards, Werner for English, Bezos for science. Next year, Bezos heads for Princeton University to study engineering. Werner, who plans to major in English, has just finished her first year at Duke University.

Werner and Bezos spend their mornings teaching, their afternoons planning for the next day's class, researching and discussing ideas.

"I learn as much as the kids do," Werner said.

Wednesday's class, about communications, included: readings from *Gulliver's Travels* and Richard Adams' *Watership Down*, three newspaper articles (about bass dying from pollution, about Reagan's foreign policy and about nuclear proliferation), and a short talk about the Bezos family's Apple II computer.

James Schockett enters fifth grade next year at Pinecrest Elementary. He is an eager student.

At The Dream Institute, James said, he has learned "little neat things that I really think are neat. We study about black holes in outer space. We study about stars . . . We learned that one teaspoon of a neutron star would weigh 10 billion tons."

In class, after a discussion of *Gulliver's Travels*, James clamored to make an important point: Since the Lilliputians are so tiny and Gulliver is so large, wouldn't it take several generations of Lilliputians to decapitate Gulliver?

The Dream Institute is better than school, said James, who likes to swim and thinks he may become a doctor. "In school, you're getting a grade. Whenever you're getting a grade for something, you always feel slightly pressured."

Merrell Maschino, James' classmate at Pinecrest, lists another advantage: "You can call him Jeff instead of Mr. Bezos. It's like having a big brother teach you."

Bezos and Werner charge $150 for the two-week session, taught out of Bezos' par-

ents' house at 13720 SW 73rd Ave. They gear the course to fifth-grade students. Werner said, "because we decided that age is pretty creative, but also intelligent enough to understand how things work."

Teachers often underestimate their students' abilities, Bezos and Werner say, and they are careful not to do the same.

Said Werner: "You have to shock them into thinking they can do more than they think they can."

Jeff Bezos, on the camera, zooms in on Ursula Werner, James Schockett, Mark Bezos and Howard Greenman.

TRISH ROBB Miami Herald Staff

This 1982 photo from the *Miami Herald* shows teenagers Jeff Bezos and Ursula Werner conducting their DREAM Institute. The ten-day course cost $150 and taught its young students how to operate a camera and interpret books such as *Gulliver's Travels*, among other topics.

It was during high school that Jeff met Ursula Werner, a brilliant student in her own right who became his first serious girlfriend. Ursula would go on to attend Duke University on a full scholarship and be named a Rhodes scholar. Ursula admired Jeff's creative way of thinking and his thorough approach to matters great and small. For example, Jeff spent days getting a scavenger hunt ready as a surprise for Ursula's eighteenth birthday. He went so far as to have one of the clues tied to a railroad track and another

The DREAM Institute

The summer after graduation from high school, Jeff Bezos and Ursula Werner decided to run a summer education camp they named the DREAM Institute. DREAM was an acronym for "Directed REAsoning Methods." In a pamphlet the two created, they described the program as one that "emphasizes the use of new ways of thinking in old areas," a mind-set Bezos would put to good use when developing Amazon.

The *Miami Herald* kept tabs on Jeff after awarding him and two classmates the science prize in the Silver Knight competition among south Florida high school students. It reported on his valedictory speech and ran an article about the DREAM Institute, in which Bezos promised that at his camp, "We don't just teach them something. We ask them to apply it."

The DREAM Institute was run out of Jeff's house. Its five students in grades four, five, and six included his younger brother and sister. Jeff and Ursula charged $150 for the two-week program, which included subjects such as how to work a camera and how to limit the use of nuclear arms. The reading list included *Treasure Island*, *The Lord of the Rings*, *Watership Down*, and *Gulliver's Travels*.

tucked under a toilet bowl lid at a local Home Depot. That kind of inventiveness and attention to detail are two hallmarks of a true entrepreneurial spirit.

OFF TO PRINCETON

In the fall of 1982, Bezos headed off to Princeton University in New Jersey. Princeton is an Ivy League school and the fourth-oldest college in the United States. Bezos, a longtime admirer of physicists Albert Einstein and Stephen Hawking, planned to study theoretical physics. Theoretical physics uses mathematical models to better explain the physical world, from the smallest element to the outer reaches of space.

While at Princeton, Bezos encountered something he'd never dealt with before: students who were stronger in a subject area than he was. According to an interview Bezos gave when he was selected to become a member of the Academy of Achievement in Washington, D.C., "I just remember there was a point in this where I realized I'm never going to be a great physicist. There were three or four people in the class whose brains were so clearly wired differently to process these highly abstract concepts, so much more. I was doing well in terms of the grades I was getting, but for me it was laborious, hard work."

Instead of seeing this as a setback, Bezos pressed forward, changing his major to computer science and

Jeff Bezos attended Princeton University in Princeton, New Jersey, graduating summa cum laude in 1986. At first Bezos was a physics major, but he switched to computer science and engineering when he realized that he was never going to be a brilliant physicist.

electrical engineering. He was drawn to these fields, particularly computer science, which had interested him since he programmed that Teletype machine in elementary school.

In retrospect, this change in major proved a great choice for Bezos. It provided him with the skills and experience he'd need to revolutionize the way technology and the marketplace could interact. Bezos excelled at Princeton, becoming a member of the Phi Beta Kappa honor society before graduating summa cum laude in 1986.

CHAPTER 2

Early Jobs, Enduring Love

After graduating from Princeton, Bezos considered starting his own company. He realized, however, that he had more to learn about both business and the way the world worked. Bezos interviewed with older, established companies such as Bell Labs, Intel, and Anderson Consulting and was offered jobs each time.

Bezos turned down these jobs, instead choosing to work for Fitel, a start-up company based in New York City. Fitel got its name because its founders planned to combine the fields of finance and telecommunications to build a communications network that would make international business trading easier. Bezos was the eleventh employee hired by Fitel, and his title was manager of administration and development.

Bezos took charge of Fitel's telecommunications network, which utilized computer programs to connect stockbrokers, investors, and banks throughout the world. Bezos's background in computer science provided the expertise Fitel needed to improve its computer protocols. He ended up saving the company 30 percent over its previous communications costs.

By the age of twenty-three, Bezos was in charge of accounts for clients in such far-flung locales as England, Japan, and Australia. While he relied on high-speed computer networks for much of his work, he did get to travel to London often. Although he found his job fun and interesting, within two years he was ready to take on his next challenge.

MOVING ON

In April 1988, Bezos joined Banker's Trust, leading a six-person programming department. The department developed a software program that let a bank's clients check on their accounts at any time using a personal computer (PC). This was a huge innovation in an era when clients were used to waiting for a mailed monthly statement to find out such information.

From 1988 to 1990, Bezos worked at Banker's Trust in New York City. At age twenty-six, he became the youngest vice president in the company's history.

When Bezos was named a vice president at twenty-six, he became the youngest employee to earn that title in the history of Banker's Trust.

Some at Banker's Trust thought it was a waste of money to develop software that allowed people to check their accounts from a personal computer. At the time, only 15 percent of the population owned PCs and certain people at the company thought that the old way of doing things—storing the data on a mainframe computer and sending customers monthly reports—worked fine.

Bezos wasn't interested in the old way of doing things. He envisioned a time when PCs would be hugely popular and wanted to invent ways that those computers could handle the business needs of the next decade. By this point, Bezos wanted out of banking and what he referred to as "first-phase automation," which was simply a way of doing things better or faster.

Bezos was interested in second-phase automation, which he described in Gene Landrum's *Entrepreneurial Genius: The Power of Passion* as "more of a revolution than an evolution." In second-phase automation, people "fundamentally change the underlying business process to do things in a completely new way." Bezos sensed that Banker's Trust wasn't a place where such innovation would happen quickly. It was time to make another move in his professional life.

THE RIGHT CONNECTIONS

In December 1990, Jeff Bezos began working at D. E. Shaw & Company, an investment fund that used computer programs to make decisions about when to buy or sell stock. David Shaw, the founder of the company, had a background in computer science, having taught the subject at Columbia University in New York City. In Bezos, Shaw saw a smart, creative young man with an outgoing personality. Bezos admired Shaw as well, describing him in an interview with *Wired* magazine as "one of those people who has a completely developed left and a completely developed right brain. He's artistic, articulate, and analytical."

Shaw and Bezos both had a laid-back personal style. There was no particular dress code at D. E. Shaw, as later there would be no particular office attire required at Amazon. Through the years, Bezos's wardrobe consisted mostly of khakis and blue Oxford shirts, which became a kind of uniform for the new generation of buttoned-down entrepreneurs.

One of Bezos's most distinctive characteristics was his very loud laugh. *Time* magazine described the laugh as sounding like "a flock of Canadian geese on nitrous oxide," also known as laughing gas. This created the impression of Bezos as more nerd next door than corporate whiz kid or captain of industry, which suited the "roll up your sleeves" persona he was trying to project.

By the time he was twenty-eight, Bezos was named D. E. Shaw's youngest senior vice president, with a salary of more than $1 million a year. He supervised twenty-four employees whose job was to explore new markets in fields such as computer software, insurance, and the Internet, the latter of which was just beginning its growth spurt.

One of Jeff Bezos's distinctive characteristics is his very loud, "honking" laugh. Here, he greets fans at the Book Expo 2000 in Chicago, Illinois.

One of those employees was MacKenzie Tuttle, a fellow Princeton grad (class of 1992) and a researcher at D. E. Shaw. Bezos had been looking for a serious relationship and approached his personal life with the same energy as his professional life. He encouraged friends to set him up on as many blind dates as possible, telling them that he was looking for someone who was resourceful, a trait he'd come to admire years earlier while working on his grandfather's farm.

According to an interview with *Wired* magazine, his ideal woman was someone "who could get me out of a Third World prison," which speaks to Bezos's unique take on life. As fate would have it, true love didn't require a setup from Bezos's friends. He found his soul mate close at hand as Tuttle worked in the office right next door to Bezos. The first thing she noticed about him? His loud and distinctive laugh.

Although Tuttle worked as a researcher, her true passion was writing. She studied creative writing with Nobel Laureate Toni Morrison at Princeton University, and in 2005 she released *The Testing of Luther Albright*, her first novel. On its Web site, publisher HarperCollins described Tuttle's novel as "a harrowing portrait of an ordinary man who finds himself tested and strives not to be found wanting." Of course, the man Tuttle married in 1993 was anything but ordinary.

A STARTLING STATISTIC

While researching the Internet at D. E. Shaw, Bezos discovered a startling statistic. Web usage was increasing at the incredible rate of 2,300 percent a year! Bezos knew that anything growing at that fast a rate might seem invisible to most people one day but could be *everywhere* the next. Even though some companies had simple Web pages that listed information about the business, they were not selling items over the Internet. Bezos's goal was to be a so-called first mover in electronic business. He wanted to be the first to establish a company that sold products exclusively over the Internet.

Methodical as always, Bezos studied the top twenty mail-order businesses to determine which one might work as an Internet company. He realized that while the book business was huge, no one company dominated, and no mail-order catalog could possibly contain all the millions of titles available in a given year. Space wasn't an issue on the Internet, however, so the idea of selling books online made practical sense.

One of Bezos's impressive qualities is that he admits what he doesn't know, and he didn't know much about the book business. To remedy the situation, Bezos flew from New York to Los Angeles to spend the weekend at the 1994 annual convention of the American Booksellers Association.

The Rise of the Internet

In the early 1990s, few people were familiar with the Internet, even though the technology for an inter-connected system of computers had been in place since the late 1960s. That early system, known as ARPANET, was developed by the U.S. Department of Defense to help military personnel communicate in case the phone lines were destroyed during a natural disaster or nuclear attack. By the 1970s, a few people had purchased home computers, but the language codes and technology needed to link those computers weren't developed for another twenty years.

By the mid-1990s, two technological advances made the Internet far easier to navigate. The first advance was the use of hyperlinks—words and pictures that help computers jump to another page in a Web browser with the click of a mouse. The second advance was a Web browser known as Mosaic that worked on both PC and Mac platforms. Mosaic allowed users to retrieve text and graphics from anywhere on the World Wide Web. This made the experience far more accessible to the average person, rather than just researchers at universities and government agencies. The stage was set to make the Internet a place of business and not just a source of information.

At the convention, Bezos browsed the booths, gathering as much information as he could. He approached representatives from several book wholesalers. These are companies that sell to stores, which then sell to the public. Bezos was thrilled to find out that the book industry had one of the largest databases of any product. Because

Jeff and MacKenzie Bezos have been married since 1993 and have four children. They are pictured here attending a media and technology conference.

lists of millions of titles already existed, it would make the job of creating an online bookstore that much more streamlined.

NO REGRETS

Information in hand, Bezos discussed his plan for an online bookstore with MacKenzie. She shared his enthusiasm for this venture and offered her full support. Bezos's boss was less excited. David Shaw admired Bezos's initiative, but reminded him that he already had a lucrative career at a top firm and would be taking a huge financial risk with this start-up business. If his venture failed, Bezos would find himself without a job and likely without savings. Shaw recommended that Bezos take forty-eight hours to think about his future before making any drastic decisions.

Bezos took Shaw's advice and pictured himself looking back on his life as an old man. In an interview for his induction into the Academy of Achievement, he explained his theory of regret minimization: "Okay, now I'm looking back on my life. I want to have minimized the number of regrets I have. I knew that when I was eighty I was not going to regret having tried this. I was not going to regret trying to participate in this thing called the Internet that I thought was going to be a really big deal."

Bezos believed that most people regretted what they did not do, rather than actions they did take. It was this belief that led him to quit his job at D. E. Shaw in the middle of the year, giving up his annual bonus. Although Bezos wasn't even certain that the technology would improve at a fast enough pace for ordinary consumers to want to shop on the Internet, he was willing to take the risk.

After all his research, Bezos knew that his choice of books as a product category was solid. All he could do was move forward with MacKenzie beside him and his dreams laid out in front of him. He would later talk about how the stars seemed to align for him as he began his new life. Bezos certainly helped the stars along by providing great foresight and energy as he set out to change the face of business forever.

CHAPTER 3

A New Life Out West

In his typical fashion, Jeff Bezos put a lot of thought into picking the right city for his Internet business. He settled on Seattle, Washington, for several reasons. Bezos had a close friend who lived in Seattle and loved the city's natural beauty and proximity to sports, ranging from sailing to skiing. Seattle was also a hotbed of innovation, home to Microsoft, Adobe, Nintendo, and Starbucks, among other businesses. This meant that there would be a lot of talented computer programmers from which to choose when building his Web site. Equally important, Ingram Book Group, a large wholesale book company, was located in Roseburg, Oregon, a six-hour drive from Seattle. Having a wholesaler nearby meant that Bezos would be able to get books to his customers using same-day or overnight delivery.

Like many New Yorkers, Jeff and MacKenzie Bezos didn't own a car, so they flew to Texas over the Fourth of

In 1994, Jeff and MacKenzie Bezos moved to Seattle, Washington, to begin the Internet business that would become Amazon. Jeff Bezos chose Seattle for its natural beauty and because other innovative companies such as Microsoft and Starbucks had Seattle as their base.

July weekend of 1994 to get an old Chevy Blazer from his parents. MacKenzie took on most of the driving so that her husband could write out a thirty-page business plan for his new company. In an interview with the Academy of Achievement, Bezos stated that "[t]he reality will never be the plan, but the discipline of writing the plan forces you to think through some of the issues and to get sort of mentally comfortable in the space…So that's the first step."

EMPLOYEE NUMBER ONE

Another stop on the way to Seattle was San Francisco, where Bezos interviewed possible vice presidents of engineering. These were the people who would create the technology to get the Internet store up and running. One of those interviewees was Shel Kaphan, who is considered employee number one at Amazon. According to Bezos, Kaphan is the single most important person in the history of the company.

Originally from Santa Cruz, California, Sheldon "Shel" Kaphan had a B.A. degree in mathematics from the University of California, Santa Cruz. Before he met Bezos, Kaphan had worked at Kaleida Labs, a joint venture between Apple Computers and IBM that was ultimately unsuccessful. Throughout his career, Kaphan had been involved in several failed start-ups, so he was a bit wary of joining another new business. He liked Bezos's idea, however, as well as his down-to-earth and affable personality, so he decided to become part of the team. Given Kaphan's contribution to the company, this was a very promising development for Bezos.

Before arriving in Seattle, Bezos called a lawyer recommended by a friend to have the company incorporated.

The original name was Cadabra, as in "abracadabra," a term used in magic. The lawyer misheard Bezos and thought he said "cadaver," which means a dead body, and wondered why anyone would call a company by that name. Bezos incorporated under Cadabra to keep things moving, but knew he would have to change the name before too long.

When Bezos considered a new name, he knew he needed one that began with the letter "A." Yahoo!—the most popular search engine at the time—listed results alphabetically, and Bezos wanted his business near the top. He settled on Amazon.com, after the biggest river on Earth, one with many different branches. The new name wasn't officially registered until February 9, 1995.

IN THE GARAGE

Bezos rented a small house in Bellevue, Washington, a Seattle suburb. He wanted to start his business in the garage of the house, just like the founders of Microsoft and Apple. This detail shows both Bezos's sense of history and his optimism, for he wanted to be able to tell his own garage start-up tale once Amazon became successful. To hold the company computers, he and his team built inexpensive tables and desks made from doors bought at Home Depot.

In time, the Bezos family would own several grand homes, including a waterfront estate in Washington, three linked apartments in New York City, and a 12,000-square-foot (1,115-square-meter) mansion in Beverly Hills, California. At the start, however, Bezos was focused solely on getting his Internet business off the ground.

Along with Shel Kaphan, Bezos hired Paul Barton-Davis, a programmer associated with the University of Washington's computer science and engineering department. This was a time when even the most basic codes for a Web site had to be written by programmers, a tedious process that Kaphan likened to trying to empty a swimming pool with a straw. MacKenzie Bezos was in charge of bookkeeping, accounting, running errands, and handling the phones.

CONNECTING WITH CUSTOMERS

Amazon was the first Internet retailer, so Bezos and his programmers had to create a completely new way of doing business. Bezos knew that if he didn't make his Web site user-friendly, the entire operation would fail. Customers had to be able to navigate throughout the online store, choose what they wanted to buy, purchase those items, and receive what they bought in a short amount of time. Up until this point, people who were not technologically savvy were using the Internet primarily for e-mail. Getting the average consumer to take part in electronic commerce (e-commerce) required a customer interface that had never been seen before.

Brick-and-mortar stores like Barnes & Noble were rivals of Amazon. In time some, like Borders, would close their doors for good while Amazon continued to thrive.

While brick-and-mortar stores like Barnes & Noble had inventories, Bezos and his employees had lists: lists of books that were in stock or out of stock. Lists of various suppliers and of books that were in print, out of print, or soon to be printed. Lists of customer addresses and shipping information. Every bit of this information had to be compiled into workable databases in order for Amazon to have a chance at success. Bezos, Kaphan, Barton-Davis, and two other employees were determined to do the job right.

All of this work took place in the crowded garage office, with a tangle of extension cords running from electrical outlets in the house. The crew moved back and forth between computer stations, working through the winter with the help of two small space heaters. The workspace was so small that any meetings had to take place at a local Barnes & Noble, which would soon become a rival of Amazon.

INVESTING IN THE FUTURE

If creating the Web site was one big concern, money was another. Bezos invested the initial $25,000 in the company from his own savings. In November 1994, he added $29,000 to that investment. Beginning a company takes a great deal of money, however, and it soon became clear that this amount wouldn't carry them through.

GREAT INNOVATIONS

Jeff Bezos wasn't just a pioneer in creating an Internet bookseller; his company also created many of the innovations that consumers take for granted today. Throughout the years, these have included:

The shopping cart: Like an actual shopping cart, Amazon's virtual shopping cart offered a place to store items without having to commit to buying them.

One-click shopping: This technology allowed Amazon to record a customer's name, address, and shipping and billing information (including credit card numbers) in a secure manner. When visiting the site at a future date, the customer could make purchases with a single click, streamlining the shopping experience in order to save time.

Customer reviews: Amazon encouraged users of its Web site to submit reviews of books (and later, other items) that were both positive and negative. The goal was to ensure that customers trusted Amazon to give them honest feedback so that they wouldn't be tempted to shop elsewhere. The ability to read and submit reviews made customers feel like part of a larger community, which helped build customer loyalty.

E-mail confirmation: Amazon was the first to offer e-mail notification when a purchase was made and another e-mail when that purchase was shipped, a service nearly every online retailer now provides.

Amazon Prime: As a way of rewarding loyal customers, Amazon offered guaranteed two-day shipping on many items for a yearly fee of $79. Bezos was pleased with the increase in sales resulting from this program. Following his lead, other retailers began giving their customers special shipping deals and discounts.

Bezos turned to his mother and father, two of his biggest supporters. Although Mike Bezos knew nothing about the Internet, he knew that his son wouldn't start any venture without having a detailed plan for the future. Bezos was honest with his parents. He told them that according to his calculations, an Internet business had about a 10 percent chance of succeeding. Given his excellent track record in business, Bezos gave himself a 30 percent chance at success. He was clear that his parents should not invest unless they were prepared to lose their money. Despite these less-than-great odds, his parents bought $300,000 worth of shares in Amazon, risking most of their savings

**Welcome to Amazon.com
Books!**

*One million titles,
consistently low prices.*

(If you explore just one thing, make it our personal notification service. We think it's very cool!)

SPOTLIGHT! -- AUGUST 16TH

These are the books we love, offered at Amazon.com low prices. The spotlight moves **EVERY** day so please come often.

ONE MILLION TITLES

Search Amazon.com's million title catalog by author, subject, title, keyword, and more... Or take a look at the books we recommend in over 20 categories... Check out our customer reviews and the award winners from the Hugo and Nebula to the Pulitzer and Nobel... and bestsellers are 30% off the publishers list...

EYES & EDITORS, A PERSONAL NOTIFICATION SERVICE

Like to know when that book you want comes out in paperback or when your favorite author releases a new title? Eyes, our tireless, automated search agent, will send you mail. Meanwhile, our human editors are busy previewing galleys and reading advance reviews. They can let you know when especially wonderful works are published in particular genres or subject areas. Come in, meet Eyes, and have it all explained.

YOUR ACCOUNT

Check the status of your orders or change the email address and password you have on file with us. Please note that you **do not** need an account to use the store. The first time you place an order, you will be given the opportunity to create an account.

When Amazon.com first opened for business, the layout of the Web site was very simple. Technological advances have led to a more sophisticated and personalized site that greets customers by name and offers recommendations based on past purchases.

and retirement funds. They believed in their son, a faith that in time would make them extremely wealthy.

TESTING THINGS OUT AND GOING LIVE

Building the foundation for Amazon took a full six months. Along with working out deals with shippers and suppliers, Bezos and his team had to develop the software for the site and test out its programs. In the spring of 1995, they were ready to beta test the Amazon Web site.

Beta testing meant that Bezos and his team set up a so-called dummy site and asked three hundred friends and business acquaintances to play the role of shoppers. They were to go through the shopping experience and order books as if the site were real. Based on their reaction, the Amazon team would fix any bugs or other problems with the site before "going live" with an actual site and actual customers. Bezos didn't want news of Amazon to spread widely before the site was ready, so he asked his beta testers to keep what they were doing secret. He was pleased to learn that his site worked well on a range of computer platforms.

By July 16, 1995, Bezos felt confident that Amazon was ready to be shown to paying customers. He asked his three hundred beta testers to tell their friends and family that the Web site was open for business. The site itself was laid out simply, with the image of a river splitting a triangular block to form the letter "A" and beneath it the words "amazon.com: Earth's biggest bookstore." At this point, the store had one million titles available for purchase.

Bezos and his team didn't expect business to be booming at first. In fact, the team rigged a bell to go off every time there was a sale to keep their spirits high. By the end of the week, the bell was going off so much that it had to be turned off. Within a month, Amazon had shipped books to customers in every state and forty-five countries around the world.

Everyone at Amazon was thrilled that customers were using the Web site. Many of these people were early adopters, men and women who were anxious to be the first to try something new. Luck played a part as well. Within weeks of Amazon's launch, Yahoo! mentioned Amazon in its "What's Cool" feature, spurring more traffic to the site. Bezos's dream had become a reality.

CHAPTER 4

Getting Big Fast

The slogan most often associated with Jeff Bezos is "Work hard. Have fun. Make history." Bezos set out to change how the world did business, and that meant making some sacrifices along the way, particularly when it came to profits. Costs for the start-up were so high that within the first six months, Amazon lost more than $300,000, even though its profits were more than $500,000.

Bezos's idea was to grow the company quickly, before anyone else was able to copy the model Amazon had set up. This mind-set ran counter to that of most business owners, who want to cash in as quickly as they can. What Bezos was doing was revolutionary, however, and he knew it. As Robert Spector put it in the subtitle of his book *Amazon.com*, the goal of the company was to *Get Big Fast*.

With seeming nerves of steel, Bezos was willing to put everything on the line to be a true innovator. He wanted to attract as many customers as possible and then treat those customers better than any brick-and-mortar store ever had so that they would remain loyal to Amazon.

Bezos's enthusiasm was infectious. His team believed in him and in Amazon's mission to connect its customers with not only best-selling books, but also hard-to-find titles. These books might have been overlooked without the Web site's ability to search by author, keyword, subject, and publication date, as well as title. As James Marcus, an early employee, put it in his book, *Amazonia: Five Years at the Epicenter of the Dot.com Juggernaut*, "The employees of what was then essentially an online catalogue-and-fulfillment operation were intent on changing the world. Their sense of having grabbed history by the horns was almost palpable."

BEYOND THE GARAGE

Bezos always thought big. He planned to be one of the greats, like the late Apple CEO Steve Jobs and Microsoft's Bill Gates. To follow the example of Jobs and Gates, Bezos chose to start his company in a garage. Of course, he was different from those two men in a fundamental way. Bezos didn't create the hardware and operating systems that Jobs and Gates did but *used* those innovations to redefine customer service. That is one reason why Bezos has often said that one company doesn't need to fail in order for another to succeed. Without the genius of Jobs and Gates, Bezos wouldn't have been able to create Amazon. In terms of personality, Bezos was quite different from these technology pioneers as well. Both Gates and Jobs had a reputation for being prickly, while Bezos was seen as an even-tempered man who loved to laugh.

Although Bezos's early employees were programmers and not shipping clerks, everyone on the team chipped in to fulfill orders, often working late into the night. Bezos's wife, MacKenzie, pitched in as well, wrapping packages in the overcrowded office. Bezos would drive the packages to UPS at the last minute so that he could have the largest number of orders ready for shipping.

Amazon's first headquarters was in the Seattle building shown above. As Amazon was an Internet-only business, Bezos wasn't concerned with the building's appearance or the fact that it was located in an unglamorous part of town.

The small team spent many nights packing on their hands and knees until someone came up with the idea of using packing tables. In an interview with the Academy of Achievement, Bezos poked fun at himself by saying that when his back, knees, and hands started hurting from packing on the floor, his idea wasn't to get packing tables, but kneepads to make everyone more comfortable working on the floor.

"I was very serious," Bezos said, "and this person looked at me like I was the stupidest person they'd ever seen. 'I'm working for this person? This is great.'" In his defense, he said that it was very late at night when he made the comment. When the packing was finally done, Bezos would bang on the door of the UPS store, hoping those inside would feel sorry for him and let him ship things late.

A few months later, Amazon got so big that the team had to move to a commercial building. Within three years, Amazon moved four times to five different buildings as the business continued to expand. The company now owns an eleven-building complex in Seattle's South Lake Union neighborhood.

FINDING INVESTORS, LOSING MONEY

Bezos needed more money to keep his company going. In 1995, he was able to raise about a million dollars from

Customer Security

Jeff Bezos believes that Amazon's focus should be on the customer, not competitors, because competitors are not the ones sending the company money. Building trust is part of how you maintain a long-term commitment from customers, so Bezos and his team work hard to make them feel secure.

Amazon is straightforward about the data it possesses on an individual customer, and Bezos feels that this attitude garners trust. Customers are greeted by name; recommendations are made based on past selections; and if a person has already bought a product, he or she is reminded of this so that the item is not purchased twice.

Another way to earn trust is to allow negative reviews of books and other items on the Web site. Book publishers were initially wary of this, fearing it would lead to fewer sales. As is clear with his attitude toward profit, Bezos is comfortable taking the long view and believes that honesty will pay off in customer loyalty over time. Amazon does have a sophisticated program to look for review abuse (people posting fake reviews, for example) using a formula similar to one used to spot credit card fraud.

Of course, Amazon uses the latest security software available, although Bezos believes that there will always be concerns about Internet security, just as there will always be crime in the world. The bad guys are getting better at hacking into software, so the good guys have to find better ways to prevent it, too.

various investors impressed by Amazon's business plan. In keeping with his business model, all the funds went back into making Amazon as easy to use as possible. Innovations like the shopping basket, e-mail confirmation, and keeping track of previous purchases were part of what Bezos and his programmers called "frictionless shopping." This referred to shopping that took little time or effort on the part of the customer. Developing the programs to make these features available with a few clicks of a mouse required ingenuity and money, sinking the company even further into debt.

Still, Bezos wasn't discouraged. In 1996, the *Wall Street Journal* published a front-page article about Amazon titled "How Wall Street Whiz Found a Niche Selling Books on the Internet." The newspaper called Amazon "an underground sensation for thousands of book lovers around the world." The writer from the *Journal* made Amazon sound like an exciting and vibrant company that was right in line with what consumers wanted. The day the article appeared, Amazon's sales doubled, and they continued to climb. Bezos had faith that with all this growth, profits would come somewhere down the line. The article alerted the competition about Amazon's success, too. Barnes & Noble, which was the leading bookstore chain, set about designing its own Web site.

INSIDE AMAZON

What was it like to work at Amazon in those early days? In his book, *Amazonia: Five Years at the Epicenter of the Dot.com Juggernaut*, James Marcus reminds readers that when he started working at Amazon in 1996, the Internet was still somewhat confusing to most Americans and that Amazon, while gaining in popularity, was nowhere near the giant that it is today.

Marcus, who worked as an editor—before customer reviews and automated software made much of his job obsolete—was employee number fifty-five at Amazon. Bezos interviewed Marcus himself and is described by the editor as being a "likeable and normal person" with an "explosive laugh." Marcus even got an occasional glimpse of the boss's wife, who headed up the payroll department in those early days.

Bezos's interview process included asking the applicant to describe something complicated as simply as possible: for example, a way to determine the number of gas stations in Texas or windows in New York City. There was no way the interviewee could get the right answer to such a difficult question. What Bezos wanted to see was the applicant's thought process, how clever he or she was at coming up with some reasonable number. Marcus states that this was typical for a company that believed in quantifying everything and did its best to "record every move a visitor [to Amazon] made, every last click and twitch of mouse."

Bezos believed that the early employees at a workplace had a great impact on its culture. They either embraced that culture and stayed or rejected it and left. That's why he was so careful about his hiring practices. Bezos preferred to interview dozens of people and hire no one, rather than hire someone who would have a negative influence on his fledgling company.

Despite its seriousness of purpose, the atmosphere at Amazon was hardly stuffy. Dogs were allowed on the premises, and employees dressed casually and worked at simple door-like desks similar to the one Bezos had fashioned for his garage office. Marcus, who decided to join the team, describes the atmosphere as "like Spring Break in a cool climate."

Bezos took his company public on May 15, 1997, offering three million shares at $18 a share. Amazon raised $54 million by selling shares of its stock.

Marcus's work agreement included options to buy Amazon stock, though he was warned that the company might never go public with its stock, in which case his shares would be worthless. Another interesting part of the contract was the confidentiality clause, which was meant to keep the algorithms—or set of rules—that governed Amazon's programs a secret. There was also a clause about job-related stress that prohibited any employee from suing Amazon if the pace and pressure got to be too much. As Marcus put it: "If you go crazy on the job, the company won't pay to patch you up."

GOING PUBLIC

In the opening months of 1997, Amazon's sales totaled $16 million, more than all of the company's sales in 1996. Amazon had 340,000 customers, and the site was known in 100 countries. Even with all the success, Amazon lost $2.97 million in the first three months of 1997 and a startling $9 million altogether. The need to increase inventory, keep prices low, pay suppliers, and expand both warehouse and office space contributed to Amazon's mounting debt.

Bezos decided that in order to raise more money, Amazon had to go public. "Going public" means that a company offers shares to anyone who might want to invest in it. The process begins by making an initial public offering (IPO) of a certain number of shares at a certain price. Right before Amazon was about to go public, however, Barnes & Noble hit it with a lawsuit.

The suit stated that the company made two false claims. One claim was that Amazon was "Earth's biggest bookstore," according to its Web site. Barnes & Noble called this untrue because Amazon wasn't an *actual* bookstore at all. The second claim was that Amazon stocked five times as many titles as any Barnes & Noble store. According to Barnes & Noble, this was false because Amazon's warehouse stocked only a few hundred titles, even though, like Barnes & Noble, it could obtain many other titles.

The lawsuit was settled out of court with neither side admitting blame or paying out any money in damages. Damage was done to Amazon's reputation, however, said some analysts who watched the story play out. They dubbed Amazon "Amazon.toast" and predicted that giant Barnes & Noble would soon crush the upstart company under its feet.

Fearless as ever, Bezos took Amazon public on May 15, 1997, offering three million shares at $18 per share. According to James Marcus in *Amazonia: Five Years at the Epicenter of the Dot.com Juggernaut*, some employees loaded ticker software onto their computers that allowed them to watch as the stock price went up a few points before stabilizing. Later, Bezos came on over the loudspeaker and announced, "Today we made history at Amazon.com."

Going public raised $54 million for the company. Employees at Amazon made money, too. On the day of the initial public offering, some employees danced around their TVs, crying out, "We're rich, we're rich!" A few months later, Marcus sold some of his shares for more than $53,000.

There would still be many ups and downs for Amazon and its shareholders as the business continued to pursue growth. Due to its constant reinvestment in the company, Amazon wouldn't have a full profitable year until 2003. Yet it ended 1997 with sales of $147 million and a growth rate of 3,000 percent. This was far bigger than the 2,300 percent growth rate that had spurred Bezos's initial interest in the Internet back in 1994.

CHAPTER 5

More Than Just Books

In the spring of 1998, Amazon added CDs to its list of items available for purchase. It was able to offer a far greater selection than other stores at a much lower price. It also gave customers the chance to listen to samples of hundreds of thousands of recordings at the Web site before making a purchase.

By October of that year, Amazon was the biggest seller of music online. It would continue to add product categories each year, including DVDs, toys, home goods, outdoor furniture, cookware, clothing, and sporting goods. This expansion was in line with Bezos's belief that he was selling a service, not a product. Selling books was limiting. But services could be about anything, giving Amazon ample opportunity for growth.

Amazon was moving into other countries as well. Beginning in Germany in the fall of 1998, Amazon would expand into the United Kingdom, France, and Japan by

In 1997, Bezos hand-delivered a package to a man in Japan who opened Amazon's one millionth customer account. Flying to Japan to deliver the package, signed by every Amazon employee, drew positive publicity to a company that would not have a full profitable year until 2003.

the year 2000. Bezos went so far as to hand-deliver one Japanese family's first package from Amazon. The video-tape of that delivery was shown all over Japanese televi-sion, which gave Amazon a great publicity boost. Amazon now maintains Web sites in China, Italy, and Canada, too, and ships many items internationally.

With all this growth, the company needed more dis-tribution centers. Five new facilities were approved in 1998 for a 1999 opening. These were linked to the Seattle center and to one in Delaware that had opened in 1997. Building these distribution centers (also called warehouses or fulfillment centers) would cost $200 million, another example of Bezos putting all his profits back into the business.

As Amazon continued to expand, additional facilities were added. The company now has approximately fifty fulfillment centers in North America, Europe, and Asia, with more planned for the future. A few facilities have closed in recent years, however. The closings are often due to Amazon's disputes with states over collecting sales tax from customers, even though it isn't considered a retail operation. Amazon had attempted to get a referendum on the California ballot to eliminate sales tax for online sellers entirely. In September 2011, however, California legislators agreed to hold off on taxing Amazon's customers for at least another year. In return, Amazon agreed to drop its fight against the current sales tax law in that state.

According to an article in the *Arizona Republic*, the inventory at these distribution centers is managed by "increasingly sophisticated software that tells the company what to order, where to store it, what to charge for it, and when to mark it down to move it out." Warehouse workers in Arizona walk 18 to 20 miles (29 to 32 km) each shift as they haul merchandise through the giant warehouse. There are three such centers in Phoenix, totaling more than 2.5 million square feet (232,258 sq m).

NEW INVESTMENT

By the end of 1998, Amazon was the third-largest bookseller in the country, behind giants Barnes & Noble and Borders. Stock in the company continued to go up and down—its high on December 15 was more than $300, for example, while its low on that day was $243—but its market value was higher than many established companies.

All these factors drew the interest of private equity firms, which are firms that invest in companies that have great potential but are struggling financially. An equity firm gains a percentage of stock in return, hoping that the stock gains value over time.

The California firm of Kleiner Perkins Caufield & Byers invested $8 million in Amazon in return for approximately 13 percent of the company's stock. While this investment gave Bezos and his team a much-needed boost, costs continued to soar as the company focused on improving customer service. It took a lot of money to turn "Earth's biggest bookstore" into what Hoovers.com, a business research company, and many others referred to as "Earth's biggest anything store."

Amazon employees work at a warehouse in Germany in 2010. Amazon runs about fifty fulfillment centers in North America, Europe, and Asia, with plans for additional facilities in the future.

Part of this growth involved the use of automated personalization software, which was designed to create a home page tailored to the tastes of each individual shopper. According to James Marcus in *Amazonia: Five Years at the Epicenter of the Dot.com Juggernaut*, this advanced software would meet Bezos's goal of having "a unique store for every customer." While editors like Marcus had provided this service in the past, by the end of 2000, the home page was "untouched by human hands."

Around this time, the Bezos family was growing as well. Jeff and MacKenzie's son Preston was born in 2000, followed by two more boys and a daughter adopted from China. Not surprisingly, MacKenzie has said that like their father, all four children love to laugh.

GAINS AND LOSSES

Jeff Bezos never expected everything that Amazon attempted to do to be successful. In an interview with a reporter at ConsumerReports.org, he called that "an unreasonable bar," especially for a company as focused on innovation as Amazon. At its fulfillment centers, the company performs "hundreds of small experiments" to try to improve customer service. It is this willingness to try and fail and try again that has kept Amazon moving forward for close to two decades.

In 1999, Bezos began an online auction area to go head-to-head with the extremely successful eBay. Pierre

Omidyar, the founder of eBay, had more than three million customers on his Web site. Omidyar's site was profitable, too, unlike Amazon, which would not have a profitable year until 2003. Bezos decided to auction off items for charity to give this new area of interest a publicity boost. The items included the first wooden desk he made for himself when starting up Amazon, which his mother bought for $30,100. Some financial analysts predicted that Amazon's auction business would be a huge success.

It wasn't. In fact, in *Amazonia: Five Years at the Epicenter of the Dot.com Juggernaut*, Marcus calls it "the company's first high-profile pie in the face." Part of the problem was that eBay had come up with the idea of an auction site first as Amazon had done with the online book business. These companies developed a very loyal customer base that was hesitant to try anything new unless that loyalty was betrayed.

Another problem was with the matching function of Amazon's software, which was dependent on keywords. With all these auction items suddenly flooding the site, there were bound to be mismatches based on these keywords. For example, if a customer looked up a children's book such as *The Subtle Knife*, he or she was offered switchblades to bid on, hardly the appropriate object. Other inappropriate items were available on the site as well, making it seem as though Amazon could not control what the auction dealers were offering. For

Time Magazine's
Person of the Year

Every year the editors of *Time* magazine select an individual to be named "Person of the Year." This person is someone they believe has had a tremendous impact on the world, whether negative or positive. U.S. presidents, astronauts, and world leaders have appeared in this highly anticipated issue of the magazine.

In 1999, Jeff Bezos was named *Time* magazine's Person of the Year. At thirty-five, he was the fourth-youngest person ever to appear on the cover. Only Charles Lindbergh, who was twenty-five when he flew across the Atlantic on a solo flight in 1927; Queen Elizabeth II, who ascended to the throne of England and the United Kingdom at twenty-six in 1952; and thirty-four-year-old civil rights leader Martin Luther King Jr., honored in 1963, were younger than Bezos. This was very celebrated company for the young entrepreneur.

The cover of *Time* showed Bezos's head in a packing box, surrounded by books on one side and a sprinkling of Styrofoam packing peanuts throughout. In the feature article on Bezos, he was called the "king of cybercommerce." The editors of the

Time magazine named Jeff Bezos Person of the Year in 1999. At thirty-five, he was the fourth-youngest person to receive this recognition.

magazine reminded their readers that there was a time when few believed that online selling would be successful. Bezos, however, had a "vision of the online retailing universe that was so complete, his Amazon.com site so elegant and appealing, that it became from Day One the point of reference for anyone who had anything to sell online." This quote highlighted Bezos's extraordinary insight and fearlessness when starting his company. As *Time* put it, Bezos "helped build the foundation of our future."

a company obsessed with customer service, this was a huge misstep.

Although Bezos was committed to making Amazon's auction area a success, a year after eBay opened it had nearly 58 percent of the market compared to Amazon's just over 3 percent. By 2001, Amazon's percentage was a measly 2 percent, a failure to be sure. The auction area, which at one point partnered with the famous auction house Sotheby's, ended up closing altogether.

Other missteps included Amazon creating an electronic greeting card category to rival Blue Mountain Arts and the purchase of a 50 percent share in Pets.com, which went out of business in 2000, filing for bankruptcy shortly thereafter. The Pets.com sock puppet, used in its TV and print ads, soon came to represent the worst excesses of the dot-com boom era. This was a time from the mid-1990s to the early 2000s when huge amounts of money were invested in businesses that hoped to make money off of the public's newfound interest in the Internet. The bubble of boom times would soon go bust.

THE BUBBLE BURSTS

By 2000, it was clear that many of the online companies formed in the mid- to late 1990s were not going to turn a profit. This made a lot of investors nervous, so they sold their stock, causing prices to drop. The value of these companies came crashing down, and many went out of business. In January 2000, Amazon's stock lost 40 percent of its value, though unlike other companies, the stock stabilized by the spring of that year. Those who sold when the stock was cheap lost a great deal of money. Among them was James Marcus, employee fifty-five at Amazon, who was no longer a millionaire by the time he left the company in 2001.

Although some financial analysts predicted the end of Amazon, Bezos never lost his optimism about the future. The company continued to grow, serving six million more customers in 2000 than in 1999. Yet for the first time, Bezos had to let a total of 1,300 employees go. He set aside stock worth $2.5 million for those who were fired.

There were other setbacks, too. In 1998, Walmart filed a lawsuit claiming that Amazon was hiring Walmart workers to find out that company's business practices. The suit was settled when Amazon agreed to reassign executives with knowledge of Walmart's computer systems to other jobs in the company. In addition, Amazon's decision to patent both its computer systems and its successful affiliates program—which gave Web site owners and bloggers a percentage of sales if they linked to Amazon—came across to some as the company acting like a bully. Yet as the business continued to weather the storms, many were impressed by the company's resilience and by its leader, whom *Forbes* magazine described as "[a] genuinely nice guy who's kept his sense of humor in the face of intense pressure."

Bezos's ability to handle pressure was tested when a helicopter in which he was one of three passengers crashed on March 6, 2003. High winds over the Texas plains caused problems for the pilot, and the main rotor of the helicopter hit a tree. The helicopter rolled over and landed in the aptly named Calamity Creek. The U.S. Border Patrol rescued the group and luckily none of the passengers suffered grave injuries.

TURNING A PROFIT

On January 28, 2004, a *New York Times* story announced that in 2003 Amazon earned a full-year profit of $35 million. Bezos's own net worth in 2003 was an estimated $2.5 billion, a huge leap for the man who had needed to borrow $300,000 from his parents to start his company.

Yet for someone like Bezos, who wanted to revolutionize the way customers worldwide did business, personal wealth was never the goal. Innovation was key. So in 2003, Amazon introduced the "Search Inside the Book" feature. This feature allowed customers to browse through a few pages of a book, though not copy or download it.

Some publishers were angered by the move, believing that it went against the copyrights they held on the books. Bezos insisted that the point of this feature was to inform customers, not to give away the contents of the book. "Search Inside the Book" proved to be quite popular, as books that offered this feature had increased sales of 9 percent compared to those that didn't.

Although Pets.com and other businesses bought by Amazon didn't do well, over the years the company acquired many successful companies, including Shopbop. com; the Internet Movie Database (IMDb); Askville (a community-based question-and-answer site); Diapers. com; and Zappos.com, the online shoe and clothing giant, for which it paid well over $800 million in 2009.

In an effort to offer as wide a selection of merchandise as possible, Amazon launched its Marketplace in 2000. The Marketplace allows outside sellers—referred to as third-party sellers—to offer their products right alongside those that Amazon sells directly. These Marketplace products now represent approximately one-third of the total units shipped by Amazon.

Using outside sellers doesn't mean that Amazon won't step in when there is a problem. When a customer ordered a workbook described by the seller as "like new" and it arrived with the worksheets filled out, she contacted the seller. When the seller didn't respond, she called Amazon, and she was given a full refund and was allowed to keep the book. It is this focus on keeping the customer happy that has led to such loyalty to Amazon and to ever-increasing sales.

CHAPTER 6

The Kindle:
Changing the Face
of Reading

In 2007, Jeff Bezos ushered Amazon into a new era of its business. The company that was known for selling books and other products was now creating its own product: the Kindle, a handheld electronic reader (e-reader) specifically designed for reading longer works of fiction and nonfiction.

According to *Newsweek*, best-selling author Annie Proulx once stated, "[n]obody is going to sit down and read a novel on a twitchy little screen. Ever." Bezos—and other manufacturers of e-readers—would go on to prove Proulx very wrong. In 2010, Amazon announced that the Kindle was the best-selling product in the *history* of the company, although Bezos and his team didn't release exact figures.

Once again, Bezos's vision of what his company could accomplish and his lifelong zeal for innovation pressed him forward. "You can always do what you should do if you're willing to put in the time and energy to develop a new set of skills," he told a reporter at CNNMoney. "If you only extend into places where your skill sets serve you, your skills will become outmoded." Bezos considers the Kindle the most important thing that Amazon has ever done and refers to those working on the device as missionaries.

A BREAKTHROUGH IN DESIGN

When the Kindle was released in 2007, electronic books had been on the market for fifteen years but had never been big sellers. Earlier versions of electronic readers

Bezos first introduced the Kindle DX, shown here, in 2009. The Kindle DX has a larger screen than the Kindle that was introduced in 2007, making the viewing of charts, textbooks, and large documents easier.

were not easy to use, and there were not many electronic books available for sale. If Amazon's Kindle was going to be a success, Bezos had to offer a device that seemed more convenient than an actual book, a tall order when people were used to reading in a more traditional format. He asked himself why he loved books and the smell of glue and ink. The answer was that those smells were linked "with all those worlds I have been transported to," he stated in a *Newsweek* interview. "What we love is the words and ideas."

The breakthrough for electronic readers came in 2006 with the development of electronic ink (e-ink). E-ink was designed to cause far less eyestrain than the LCD display on machines such as a laptop, tablet, or cell phone. In an interview on the *Charlie Rose* show, Bezos said that reading on those devices was like "reading with a flashlight flashing in your eyes." The company does offer free Kindle applications for these devices so that customers who own PCs, iPads, Blackberries, Android phones, and the like can still buy e-books through Amazon.

What made the Kindle so innovative? It was a lightweight, portable device that used wireless technology, making it possible to download e-books without having to be connected to a computer. In less than sixty seconds, customers could have not just books but also blogs, newspapers, and magazines available at their fingertips. The long battery life of the Kindle added to its appeal, as did the ability to change the font size, creating a large-print book using a button at the bottom of the keyboard. Amazon already had a large and loyal customer base from which to draw as long as the Kindle delivered on its promises.

A SHAKY START

The Kindle's release wasn't without problems. The e-reader sold out in five and a half hours, and some customers had to wait as long as six weeks for their Kindle. Bezos was forced to put an apology letter on Amazon's Web site that stated, in part, "We hope to be able to announce to you within the next few weeks that we're back in stock and that when you order a Kindle, we'll ship it to you that very same day." Amazon prided itself on its excellent customer service, so this was an embarrassment to the company at a crucial time. There were a few analysts, however, who believed that Bezos orchestrated the shortage to make it seem as if the Kindle was in higher demand than it actually was.

Reviews of the first-generation Kindle were positive overall, although some critics felt that its original asking price of $399 was too high. Prices for most e-books were set at $9.99, which Bezos thought was fair considering that readers couldn't lend out the books, give them as gifts, or resell them.

Some publishers, including Macmillan, thought the price of e-books was too low. In 2010, Amazon temporarily

The Kindle has become the best-selling product on Amazon. By the early part of 2011, more Amazon customers were choosing electronic books than print books, whether paperback or hardcover.

pulled all Macmillan e-books from its Web site before agreeing to charge $14.99, a price Amazon called "needlessly high" in a statement. The statement mentioned Macmillan's "monopoly" over its books as the reason why Amazon had no choice but to give in to its demands. It is clear from Amazon's statement, however, that Bezos was unhappy with the outcome of this conflict. At present, most new releases in Amazon's Kindle store are offered at a price of $12.99 or less.

Despite the high price of the first Kindle, within six months more than 6 percent of Amazon's book sales were Kindle downloads, and before a year was up that number was at 10 percent. The trend continued upward. By early 2011, Amazon customers were choosing electronic books more often than print books, hardcover or paperback. "We had high hopes that this would happen eventually, but we never imagined it would happen this quickly," Bezos said in a press release. "[W]e've been selling print books for fifteen years and Kindle books for less than four years." The first million-seller e-book for the Kindle was Stieg Larsson's *The Girl with the Dragon Tattoo*.

THE NEXT GENERATION

As with any entirely new system, Bezos knew that the Kindle would need improvements over time. Within a year, a second-generation Kindle was rolled out, and in 2009 the Kindle DX, an alternate version with a larger screen and more storage capacity, was released.

In the fall of 2011, Amazon introduced four new Kindles, including the Kindle Fire, a tablet with an LCD display that will be discussed in the next chapter. The new Kindle Wi-Fi is lightweight and compact enough to fit into a pocket, and it relies on a five-way button control rather than a keyboard. The Kindle Touch Wi-Fi and Kindle Touch 3G use touchscreen technology to navigate through the device. The Kindle Touch models have a feature called X-Ray that sends a second file to the Kindle when a customer downloads a book. This file contains information about the characters and settings of the book gathered from sources such as Wikipedia and Shelfari, a social networking site for readers owned by Amazon.

In addition to these three models, the earlier generation Kindle Keyboard Wi-Fi and Kindle Keyboard 3G, as well as the Kindle DX, are still available. All of these machines use black-and-white e-ink and feature page numbers, as well as the ability to download e-books from the library. Amazon Prime members now have access to a lending library, where thousands of titles, including current and past best sellers, are available to borrow for free.

College students now have the option of renting textbooks for their Kindles or for devices such as laptops or smartphones using a free, downloadable application. Students have tens of thousands of textbooks to choose from with discounts of up to 80 percent off the purchase price. The books would be available for up to 360 days, but students would have to pay for only the amount of time they used. Any notes or highlighted material from a Kindle could be kept in a remote server. This server, called a cloud drive (discussed in more detail in the next chapter), holds the notes even after the rental period expired so that they could be accessed anytime.

Along with these convenient features, the newest Kindles are also much less expensive, ranging in price from $79 for the Kindle Wi-Fi to $199 for the Kindle Fire. When announcing the new lineup of Kindles, Bezos referred to them as "premium products at non-premium prices," according to the *Washington Post*.

One inventive way Amazon offsets the price of the least expensive models is by featuring advertisements on the Kindle's screensaver and at the bottom of its home screen. Through a service called Admash, customers can download two different sponsored screensavers and vote on the one they find most appealing. Amazon then uses this information to determine which screensavers it will use in the future. There is even a feature that lets customers set preferences for sponsored screensavers based on whether they would like to see landscapes, architecture, travel images, or illustrations. As always, Amazon remains data-driven and focused on customer service.

The Kindle is not without its competitors, including products by Kobo, Sony, Barnes & Noble, and Apple. Those devices, designed primarily for reading longer works, continue to rely on black-and-white e-ink. As Bezos told a reporter from ConsumerReports.org, color e-ink "was not ready for prime time." Tablet computers like the Fire, iPad, Nook Color, and Nook Tablet that offer movies, apps, and games, as well as e-books, come with color LCD screens.

Big Mistake, Big Apology

In July 2009, Amazon deleted copies of George Orwell's *1984* and *Animal Farm* from Kindles without informing customers beforehand. Amazon stated that a company that didn't hold the rights to the books added them to the Kindle store and therefore the copies of the e-books were illegal. It seemed particularly ironic that Amazon deleted *1984*, a book about government censorship, without the say-so of its customers.

Kindle owners were upset to see the books vanish from their devices. "I never imagined that Amazon actually had the right, the authority or even the ability to delete something that I had already purchased," Charles Slater, a customer who had purchased *1984*, stated in a *New York Times* article.

In the same article, another Kindle owner voiced his frustration: "It illustrates how few rights you have when you buy an e-book from Amazon...I can't lend people books and I can't sell books that I've already read, and now it turns out that I can't even count on still having my books tomorrow."

Bezos realized that his company had made a mistake and issued an apology on Amazon's Web site. "Our 'solution' to the problem was stupid, thoughtless, and painfully out of line with our principles," he stated. "It is wholly self-inflicted, and we deserve the criticism we've received." By acknowledging the mistake, Bezos helped prevent the mishap from becoming a public relations disaster that would tarnish the company's image in the long term. Soon after Bezos made his comments, customers were offered the choice of having a different edition of the book delivered to their Kindles without charge, or receiving a check or gift certificate for $30.

Amazon introduced another innovation in the summer of 2011: the Kindle Cloud Reader. The Cloud Reader is not a machine itself, but a Web-based application that allows customers to access their books on any Web-connected device, including the iPad. No specific operating system, such as Android or Apple's iOS platform, is required. With the Kindle Cloud Reader, Amazon can link customers directly to its digital bookstore, bypassing Apple's App Store. For Amazon, this means that the company would no longer be required to pay Apple's 30 percent sales tax. At the time of its introduction, Google Chrome, Apple Safari desktop, and iOS Safari for iPhones

On September 28, 2011, Bezos introduced four new Kindles, including the Kindle Fire. According to analysts, customers pre-ordered an estimated ninety-five thousand units of the Fire on the first day it was available for sale.

and iPads were the only Web browsers supported. Other browsers would be added "in the coming months," according to a statement from Amazon.

THE DRIVING FORCE

In 2008, Jeff Bezos was named *Publishers Weekly* Person of the Year. The magazine viewed Bezos as "the driving force behind one of the industry's most dynamic, if sometimes controversial, companies." The controversy stemmed from what the magazine viewed as many publishers' "love-hate" relationship with Amazon. While many spoke on the record about Amazon's influence and rapid growth, off the record others criticized the company's aggression when it came to working out terms with various publishers.

Some publishers felt squeezed by Amazon's push to get the lowest price possible, which they would then pass on to consumers. One executive complained that in a business like publishing that had low profit margins—the ratio of profit to total sales—there wasn't much margin to give. While Bezos acknowledged that his relationship with some publishers was better than with others, he told *Publishers Weekly* that overall he was "extremely pleased with how supportive publishers have been of our endeavors."

As Amazon continued to expand, those endeavors reached into most areas of the book industry. The company acquired AbeBooks, a major used-book retailer; Audible.com, an audiobooks company; and Lexcycle, which makes an e-reading application for Apple's iPhone.

With CreateSpace, authors are able to self-publish with Amazon. CreateSpace offers the manufacturing-on-demand model, which means that products are made as customers order them, rather than Amazon requiring that a minimum amount be produced. This applies not only to books, but also to CDs, DVDs, video downloads, and Amazon MP3s.

AmazonEncore is a program for self-published books that earned good reviews on Amazon and other sites but didn't sell in large numbers. Published by Amazon under the AmazonEncore imprint, a book is offered in paperback, e-book, and audio book formats. The first book to be published in this manner was a fantasy title, *Legacy*, whose author, Cayla Kluver, was just sixteen when she self-published her novel.

A few other books have been published under the AmazonEncore imprint, including one by J. A. Konrath, best-selling author of the Jacqueline "Jack" Daniels thrillers. A *Time* magazine article once questioned whether Amazon was taking over every facet of publishing. While the writer concluded that Amazon was unlikely to drive traditional publishers out of the book business, Bezos's company continues to be a powerful force in the industry.

CHAPTER 7

Always Moving Forward

Jeff Bezos has often said that he is not in the habit of talking about the future. It is clear that he thinks about the future, however, as he is involved in a wide range of projects that touch the very core of twenty-first-century living.

In 2010, Amazon invested $175 million in LivingSocial, a competitor to Groupon, the coupon Web site that offers daily deals to its customers. Bezos has also partnered with Kleiner Perkins Caufield & Byers—the firm that made an early investment in Amazon—as well as Facebook's Mark Zuckerberg and Zynga's Mark Pincus to create a fund focused on social media.

"I think it's fun to work in golden ages," Bezos said to a reporter at Portfolio.com. "And this probably is the golden age of social apps."

Amazon developed a new Web site named MYHABIT. com that offers discount designer clothing for men, women,

In 2006, Amazon launched endless.com, its own shoes and accessories Web site that offers free shipping and returns. In 2011, endless.com began offering a free app for the iPhone that allows customers to shop on the go.

and children. MYHABIT.com bills itself as a "fashion and lifestyle" Web site. Users are sent daily e-mails highlighting which high-end items are currently on sale.

CLOUD COMPUTING

Since 2006, Amazon has offered its customers a service known as cloud computing. On the Web site, Amazon refers to its Cloud Drive as "your hard drive in the cloud." The Cloud Drive uses Amazon's own remote servers, rather than a local server or personal computer, to securely store a customer's music, videos, documents, and photos. The Cloud Drive allows data to be accessed from any location where an Internet connection is available.

Large companies such as Netflix and pharmaceutical giant Eli Lilly & Company use Amazon's cloud computing services to store data. Many small businesses use the service as well, although Amazon has competition from companies such as Google, Dell, and most recently, Apple. At a 2010 shareholders' meeting, Jeff Bezos stated that in time Amazon's Web services could be as big as the company's e-commerce business.

Unfortunately, there are those who will use a service like cloud computing to cause harm. In April 2011, hackers used Amazon's Elastic Computer Cloud (EC2) to attack Sony's online entertainment systems, leading to a shutdown of Sony's PlayStation Network and other services for nearly a month.

While Amazon's servers were not hacked, the intruders used a fake name to set up an account that ended up compromising more than one hundred million Sony customers. The convenience and relatively low cost of cloud computing is a plus for individuals and small businesses. Yet these same factors mean that anyone can set up an anonymous account, making it difficult to find the "bad guys" in the mix.

WikiLeaks is one Web site that used Amazon's remote servers for a time. WikiLeaks' editor in chief, Julian Assange, released classified material about the U.S. military and diplomatic service. Some officials, including Secretary of State Hillary Rodham Clinton and Senator Joseph Lieberman, thought this action put people's lives in danger. Not long after Lieberman's criticism, Amazon dropped WikiLeaks as a customer.

Some believed Bezos bowed to government pressure in the WikiLeaks case, though an Amazon spokesman called these claims "inaccurate" in a statement released to the press. The spokesman did acknowledge that Amazon faced "large-scale" attacks after hosting WikiLeaks on its servers, but that these attacks were "successfully defended against."

THE KINDLE FIRE

When Jeff Bezos unveiled the Kindle Fire in September 2011, it drew immediate comparisons to Apple's iPad.

A Strong Belief in Giving Back

Bezos and his relatives, as well as employees of Amazon, head up many charitable endeavors. Jackie and Mike Bezos established the Bezos Family Foundation. They serve on the board of directors, along with Jeff and MacKenzie, and Jeff's brother and sister and their spouses. According to its Web site, the foundation supports "rigorous, inspired learning environments for young people, from birth through high school, to put their education into action."

Through its program Students Rebuild, the foundation invited young people from more than thirty-seven countries to make paper cranes in support of those devastated by the earthquake in Japan. This effort triggered $500,000 in funds from the Bezos Family Foundation and an anonymous donor. Among its many other projects, the foundation has also given a $5 million gift to the University of Washington's Developing Minds Project to study how and when young children learn.

In 2007, Bezos himself paid $3.98 million for one of seven copies of *The Tales of Beedle the Bard* by Harry Potter author J. K. Rowling. The money went to Rowling's charity, Children's Voice.

Amazon employees can give to nonprofits through the company's payroll deduction program, and many employees throughout the country have volunteered in their own communities. These efforts include:

- Walking as a team to raise funds for the American Cancer Society

- Collecting hundreds of pounds of food for a food bank and hundreds of books for a children's hospital

- Donating toys to children's charitable organizations

- Collecting donations for the Humane Society's programs in support of the compassionate treatment of animals, as well as community education and adoption promotion

The Fire, a mobile device with a 7-inch (17.8 centimeter) LCD color touchscreen and 8 gigabytes of memory, is a much different machine from the iPad, however. To begin with, the Fire's price tag of $199 is far lower than the $499 starting price for the iPad. In addition, while the iPad offers more memory, 3G connectivity, a built-in camera, and other features, the Fire is focused on helping

Amazon consumers access their company's content. This includes a huge storehouse of eighteen million books, movies, TV shows, songs, and magazines, as well as thousands of Android apps and games.

"I think of it as a service," Bezos stated in the *New York Times*. "Part of the Kindle Fire is of course the hardware, but really, it's the software, the content, it's the seamless integration of those things."

The Fire is built on Google's Android software, though that framework is under a custom-built layer designed by Amazon. The Fire offers Amazon's own Web browser called Amazon Silk, as well as the ability to store content on its Cloud Drive. Amazon Prime members can also stream thousands of movies and television shows for free on the Fire, although the Fire is not the only device on which this content can be viewed.

As the Fire has just been released, its long-term success remains to be seen. Few are betting against Bezos, however, and some analysts expect that Amazon will sell five million devices by the end of 2011. A leader with a track record like his, especially one as patient and determined as Bezos, seems as close to a sure thing as one is likely to find.

HEADING INTO SPACE

For the boy who once envisioned becoming an astronaut, the fact that spaceflight remains one of Bezos's passions should come as no surprise. According to its Web site, the team at Blue Origin, Bezos's aerospace company, is developing a "vertical take-off, vertical landing vehicle designed to take a small number of astronauts on a sub-orbital journey into space." The first step in that process was the launch and landing of the spacecraft *Goddard*, which took place in west Texas on November 13, 2006.

Many friends and family were present to cheer the team as the *Goddard* had its initial unmanned launch. There was food from a chuck wagon and even a bouncy castle for the kids. Bezos, never one to take himself seriously, poked fun at how he flubbed the one thing he was asked to do at the launch: "My only job...was to open the champagne and I broke the cork off the bottle :)" he is quoted as saying on Blue Origin's Web site.

At the site, there is video of the *Goddard* taking off and landing. The *New York Times* described the *Goddard* as a vehicle with a "science-fiction sleekness" that took off and landed with a "loud whooshing sound." According to the *Times*, there are several companies working on spacecraft, including one owned by Richard Branson, the billionaire founder of Virgin Atlantic Airways.

MONEY FROM NASA

In April 2011, the National Aeronautics and Space Administration (NASA) distributed $269 million to four private

NASA allotted money to four companies that developed their own spacecraft, including the McDonnell Douglas Reusable Launch Vehicle (RLV), shown here. Blue Origin's *Goddard* spacecraft is similar in design, and it had its first unmanned launch on November 13, 2006.

companies and $22 million of that total went to Blue Origin to work on its space capsule. The company also received $3.7 million from NASA in 2010.

Besides its facility in west Texas, Blue Origin has a 280,000-square-foot (26,0123 sq m) headquarters in Kent, Washington, to work on its spacecraft. Blue Origin's goal is to have an unmanned suborbital flight (a flight that goes into space but not around Earth) in 2011 and a manned flight in 2012.

In August 2011, an unmanned Blue Origin spacecraft veered out of control during a suborbital test flight and had to be destroyed. Ground personnel lost contact with the craft while it was flying faster than the speed of sound at an altitude of 45,000 feet (13,716 m). The automated safety system shut off all thrust on the spacecraft, leading to its destruction. On the Blue Origin Web site, Bezos acknowledged in a statement that this was "[n]ot the outcome any of us wanted," but said that the team had "signed up for this to be hard."

The latest round of money being distributed is part of what NASA refers to as its Commercial Crew Development program. This program is betting on

Bezos's energy, optimism, and sense of fun have helped him handle the ups and downs that come with running a huge company. He has an unwavering faith in his ability to have a positive impact on the world.

the fact that commercial companies will have more success than NASA in getting people to and from orbit.

According to the *New York Times*, the director of the program hoped to have private providers flying astronauts to the International Space Station by the "middle part of the decade." With the Space Shuttle Program recently ended, NASA is looking for alternate ways to continue to send astronauts into space.

Some in Congress have their doubts about the commercial crew approach and have insisted on more money for NASA to develop its own rocket and capsule as a backup. Given the agency's tight budget, however, it seems clear that Blue Origin and other private companies will have a large stake in the future of spaceflight in the United States.

A NEW SOURCE OF ENERGY

Another area of focus for Bezos is nuclear energy. He was part of a $32.5 million investment in General Fusion, a Canadian start-up. The money goes toward General Fusion's development of Magnetized Target Fusion Technology, which the company claims will offer a clean, safe, and relatively cheap source of power with zero radioactive waste.

General Fusion is a small company, headed up by physicist Michel Laberge. Jeff Bezos is not one to shy away from taking risks, so it suits his personality to invest in a fifty-person team going up against thousands of scientists backed by billions of dollars.

Laberge is trying to do something new by causing a fusion reaction that creates more energy than it uses. He told a reporter at CNN.com that his "aha" moment came when he thought of creating "a precision controlled piston that hammers giant shock waves into a magnetized sphere—slamming atoms together hard enough to fuse and create energy."

Other companies are using huge lasers in hopes of finding a breakthrough in fusion technology, which costs a great deal more money. Laberge believes that his way of creating energy is far cheaper and more efficient. As he told CNN.com, "Glorified jackhammers are a lot cheaper than lasers."

If General Fusion is able to achieve this process, called net gain fusion—it hopes to do so on an experimental level by 2012—it could have a huge impact on the future of energy technology. To create a source of energy that is pollution-free and plentiful would limit North Americans' dependence on foreign oil and have a positive effect on climate change. Little wonder that a man as driven as Bezos would want to invest in a company that is trying to accomplish something so revolutionary.

NO LIMITS

In 2010, Jeff Bezos gave the baccalaureate remarks at Princeton University, his alma mater. He talked about the technological and scientific advances that the class of 2010 would bear witness to as the human race continued to astonish itself. "We'll invent ways to generate clean energy and a lot of it," Bezos said. "Atom by atom, we'll assemble tiny machines that will enter cell walls and make repairs. In the coming years, we'll not only synthesize [life] but we'll engineer it to specifications." Bezos believed that great minds like Mark Twain, Jules Verne, Sir Isaac Newton, and Galileo Galilei would have loved to be alive at this point in history.

Bezos himself made history by using his brilliant mind to turn an online bookseller into a worldwide phenomenon. He is one of the richest and most influential leaders in business, and Amazon continues to thrive while many other companies, most recently Borders, a rival bookseller, have had to shut down for good.

Yet Bezos is not viewed as a ruthless man. He is no pushover to be sure, but in his baccalaureate remarks he cautioned the class of 2010 against choosing cleverness over kindness. He commented that cleverness was a gift, while kindness was a choice. "You can seduce yourself with your gifts if you're not careful," he said. "[A]nd if you do, it will probably be to the detriment of your choices."

Bezos has made many hard choices in pursuit of his dreams. From the time he was a three-year-old trying to take apart his crib with a screwdriver, this unique individual has followed his own path with remarkable fortitude and optimism. He sees no limits for his company, his country, or for mankind in general. Whether delving into new fields such as aerospace and alternative energy or perfecting the day-to-day operations of Amazon, Jeff Bezos has made it his mission to have a positive impact on the world for years to come.

JEFF BEZOS

Birthdate: January 12, 1964

Birthplace: Albuquerque, New Mexico

Net worth: $18.1 billion

Ranking on *Forbes* List of Richest Americans: Thirtieth (2011)

Parents: Jackie Gise Bezos and Miguel "Mike" Bezos (stepfather)

Siblings: Half-sister Christina (born 1970) and half-brother Mark (born 1971)

Marital Status: Married to MacKenzie Tuttle Bezos since 1993

Current Residences: Seattle, Washington; New York, New York; Beverly Hills, California

Amount Paid for Mansion in Beverly Hills, California (2007): Approximately $30 million

Children: Three boys and one girl

Childhood Summers Spent: At his maternal grandfather's ranch in Cotulla, Texas

Childhood Dream Jobs: Archeologist and astronaut

Favorite Childhood Book: *A Wrinkle in Time,* by Madeleine L'Engle

Role Models: Walt Disney, Thomas Edison

Elementary School Attended: River Oaks Elementary School, Houston, Texas

High School Attended: Palmetto High School, Miami, Florida (valedictorian)

First Summer Job: Fry cook at McDonald's

Name of Summer Academy: DREAM Institute

College Attended: Princeton University, Princeton, New Jersey

College Major: Computer science and electrical engineering (switched from physics)

Year Graduated from Princeton: 1986 (summa cum laude)

First Post-Graduation Job: Fitel

Title at D. E. Shaw and Company: Senior vice president

Year Named *Time* Magazine's Person of the Year: 1999

Year Named *Publishers Weekly* Person of the Year: 2008

Amount Bezos Paid for J. K. Rowling Book to Benefit Her Children's Charity: $3.98 million.

Favorite Saying: "Work Hard. Have Fun. Make History."

Favorite Way to Relieve Stress: Laughing

Signature Style: Khaki pants, blue button-down shirt, no jacket

Distinctive Characteristic: Very loud, honking laugh

Name of Aerospace Company: Blue Origin

Blue Origin's Motto: *Gradatim Ferociter* (step-by-step, fiercely)

Fact Sheet on

AMAZON

CEO: Jeffrey Preston Bezos

Company Headquarters: Seattle, Washington

Annual Sales 2010: $34.20 billion

Employees: More than 33,000 worldwide

Where Amazon Began: In the garage of a small house in Bellevue, Washington

Employee Number One: Shel Kaphan

Original Name: Cadabra

Date Amazon.com Name Registered: February 9, 1995

Amount Mike and Jackie Bezos Invested in Amazon: $300,000

Date Company Went Live: July 16, 1995

Year One-Click Shopping Introduced: 1997

Amount Invested in Amazon by Kleiner Perkins Caufield & Byers: $8 million

Percent of Amazon Owned by Kleiner Perkins Caufield & Byers: 13 percent

Date Company Went Public: May 15, 1997

Price Per Share at IPO: $18

Amount Earned at Initial Public Offering: $54 million

Year CDs and DVDs Added to Product List: 1998

Year Toys, Electronics, Video Games, and Home
Improvement Products Added to Product List: 1999

Year Amazon.de Web Site Launched in Germany: 1999

Year Amazon.co.jp Web Site Launched in Japan: 2000

Year Amazon.fr Web Site Launched in France: 2000

Cost of Five New Warehouses Opened in 1999: $200
million

Date Amazon Stock Lost 40 Percent of Its Value:
January 2000

Total Number of Amazon Employees Let Go Due to Dot-
Com Bust: 1,300

First Full Profitable Year: 2003

Amount in Sales Earned in 2003: $35 million

Year "Search Inside the Book" Feature Added: 2003

Year Cloud Computing Introduced: 2006

Year Amazon Kindle Introduced: 2007

First Million-Seller Downloaded on Kindle: *The Girl with
the Dragon Tattoo*, by Stieg Larsson

Name of Titles Remotely Deleted from Kindles: *1984* and *Animal Farm*, both by George Orwell

Year Kindle DX Introduced: 2009

Amount Invested in LivingSocial, a competitor to Groupon in 2010: $175 million

Date E-book Sales Surpassed Print Sales at Amazon: April 1, 2011

Date Kindle Fire, Kindle Wi-Fi, and Kindle Touch (Wi-Fi and 3G) Introduced: September 28, 2011

Timeline

1964 Jeffrey Preston Bezos born on January 12 in Albuquerque, New Mexico.

1980 Wins a trip to NASA's Marshall Space Center for prize-winning essay.

1982 Named valedictorian of high school class at Palmetto High School, Miami, Florida.

1986 Graduates summa cum laude from Princeton University, Princeton, New Jersey, with a BS in electrical engineering and computer science. Accepts job at Fitel in New York City.

1988 Takes a job in the programming department at Banker's Trust in New York City. Named youngest vice president in the history of the company.

1990 Takes a job at D. E. Shaw & Company, an investment firm.

1993 Marries MacKenzie Tuttle.

1994 Moves to Seattle, Washington, to start Amazon.

1995 Registers the company name (Amazon.com) on February 9. Company "goes live" on July 16.

1996 The *Wall Street Journal* runs a positive front-page article about Amazon.

1997 Amazon goes public. Raises $54 million during initial public offering (IPO).

1998 CDs and DVDs are added to list of products sold on Amazon.

1999 Bezos is named *Time* magazine's Person of the Year. Amazon is sued for hiring away Walmart employees.

2000 Thirteen hundred Amazon employees are let go. Jeff and MacKenzie's first child, a boy named Preston, is born.

2003 Bezos survives a helicopter crash. This is the first full profitable year for Amazon, with sales of $35 million.

2006 *Goddard* spacecraft takes off and lands successfully.

2007 Amazon introduces first-generation Kindle.

2008 Bezos is named *Publishers Weekly* Person of the Year.

2009 Amazon introduces Kindle DX. Amazon buys Zappos for more than $800 million.

2010 Amazon invests $175 million in LivingSocial, a competitor to Groupon.

2011 Kindle Fire, Kindle Wi-Fi, and Kindle Touch (Wi-Fi and 3G) are introduced. Bezos invests in General Fusion, a nuclear fusion start-up.

Glossary

affable Easy to approach and get to know.

aptitude A natural ability in a certain area.

articulate Able to express oneself clearly and effectively.

atomic Having to do with small particles of matter called atoms.

booby trap A device set up by one person to surprise or trap another. Booby traps are usually set off by the presence or actions of the person being surprised.

chief executive The highest-ranking person in an organization.

colonization When people with common interests or goals settle in a particular area.

commitment A promise or a pledge to act in a particular way.

Communist government A system of government in which all social and economic activity is controlled by one political party or state.

debatable Open to dispute or questionable.

dismantle To take something apart.

entrepreneur A person who organizes, manages, and takes the risks associated with starting a new business.

founder The person who establishes a business or other type of organization.

harrowing Very disturbing or upsetting.

hovercraft A vehicle that travels over water or land on a cushion of high-pressure air.

incremental Occurring in small, gradual steps.

innovation The introduction of something new.

inquisitive Likely to ask many questions about a topic.

laborious Requiring a great amount of work.

Montessori A type of teaching instruction that allows children to learn by doing, rather than from direct instruction. Physician and educator Maria Montessori developed this method of instruction.

motto A phrase, sentence, or word that sums up the guiding principle of a person, organization, city, etc.

nuclear fusion A process during which two nuclei join to form a larger nucleus, thereby giving off energy.

optimism A belief that events will most often work out favorably.

overwhelming Enormous or overpowering.

palpable Able to be touched or felt.

personnel A group of people employed in the same business.

programmer A person who writes computer programs.

protocol A set of rules that control the formatting of data in an electronic communications system.

Rhodes scholar The winner of a scholarship named after Cecil Rhodes, a businessman and politician. Rhodes scholars study at the University of Oxford in England.

screensaver A program that displays a constantly shifting pattern on the screen when a computer is not in use.

sophisticated Describing a system, process, or piece of equipment that is complex to use.

stockbroker A person who buys and sells stocks for his or her customers.

streamlining Changing a process to make it simpler or easier to use.

summa cum laude With highest distinction or praise, used to designate a university degree awarded with the highest honors.

transformed Changed in a fundamental way.

valedictory speech A speech given by the student who ranks highest academically in a graduating class.

Wi-Fi Wireless fidelity, which refers to wireless networking technology that allows computers and other devices to communicate over a wireless signal.

For More Information

American Booksellers Association
200 White Plains Road, Suite 600
Tarrytown, NY 10591
(800) 637-0037
Web site: http://bookweb.org
This national association works to protect and encourage the interests of independently owned bookstores across the United States.

Blue Origin
21218 76th Avenue S.
Kent, WA 98032
(253) 872-0411
Web site: http://www.blueorigin.com
Blue Origin is Jeff Bezos's aerospace company. On the Web site is video of the launch and landing of the *Goddard* spacecraft.

Canada Business
(888) 576-4444
Web site: http://www.canadabusiness.ca
Canada Business offers information on starting a business,

including advice on financing, staffing, marketing, and other key issues.

Canadian Trade Commissioner Service
TCS Enquiries Service
Foreign Affairs and International Trade Canada
125 Sussex Drive
Ottawa, ON K1A 0G2
Canada
(888) 306-9991
Web site: http://www.tradecommissioner.gc.ca
The Canadian Trade Commissioner Service helps companies succeed on a global level while lowering the cost of doing business throughout the world.

Entrepreneurs' Organization
500 Montgomery Street
Alexandria, VA 22314
(703) 519-6700
Web site: http://www.eonetwork.org
Entrepreneurs' Organization provides its members with information about starting a small business and offers networking and educational opportunities.

General Fusion
108-3680 Bonneville Place
Burnaby, BC V3N 4T5

Canada

(604) 439-3003

Web site: http://www.generalfusion.com

General Fusion is the nuclear fusion start-up in which Jeff
Bezos has invested. It aims to use "magnetized target
fusion" to create a safe, sustainable, less expensive
form of energy.

National Business Association

5151 Beltline Road, Suite 1150

Dallas, TX 75254

(800) 456-0440

Web site: http://www.nationalbusiness.org

The National Business Association works to help the self-
employed and small business community achieve
their goals.

Small Business and Entrepreneurship Council

2944 Hunter Mill Road, Suite 204

Oakton, VA 22124

(703) 242-5840

Web site: http://www.sbecouncil.org

The Small Business and Entrepreneurship Council is dedi-
cated to protecting small businesses and promoting
entrepreneurship. The council works to educate poli-
cymakers, business leaders, and the public about poli-
cies that allow small businesses to thrive.

TechAmerica Foundation
601 Pennsylvania Avenue NW
North Building, Suite 600
Washington, DC 20004
(202) 682-9110
Web site: http://www.techamerica.org
TechAmerica is the leading trade association for the American technology industry. TechAmerica offers a wide range of professional development opportunities for its members.

U.S. Association for Small Business and Entrepreneurship (USASBE)
Belmont University
1900 Belmont Boulevard
Nashville, TN 37212
(615) 460-2615
Web site: http://www.usasbe.org
The USASBE fosters advancement in the four pillars of small business and entrepreneurship: education, research, outreach, and public policy. The goal of the organization is to foster the creation of new for-profit and social ventures.

U.S. Small Business Administration
409 Third Street SW
Washington, DC 20416

(800) 827-5722

Web site: http://www.sba.gov

The U.S. Small Business Administration is a government
agency that offers loans, contracts, counseling ses-
sions, and other assistance to small businesses.

WEB SITES

Due to the changing nature of Internet links, Rosen
Publishing has developed an online list of Web sites
related to the subject of this book. This site is updated
regularly. Please use this link to access the list:

http://www.rosenlinks.com/ibio/bezos

For Further Reading

Beach, Jim, Chris Hanks, and David Beasley. *School for Startups: The Breakthrough Course Guaranteeing Small Business Success in 90 Days or Less*. New York, NY: McGraw-Hill, 2011.

Bochner, Arthur, and Rose Bochner. *The New Totally Awesome Business Book for Kids*. New York, NY: Newmarket Press, 2007.

Chatzky, Jean. *Not Your Parents' Money Book: Making, Saving, and Spending Your Own Money*. New York, NY: Simon & Schuster, 2010.

Citrin, James M., and Julie Daum. *You Need a Leader— Now What? How to Choose the Best Person for Your Organization*. New York, NY: Crown Business, 2011.

Cohen, Sharon, and Rich Geller. *Amazon Income: How Anyone of Any Age, Location, and/or Background Can Build a Highly Profitable Online Business with Amazon*. Ocala, FL: Atlantic Publishing Company, 2009.

Collins, Robyn, and Kimberly Burleson Spinks. *Prepare to Be a Teen Millionaire*. Deerfield Beach, FL: HCI, 2008.

Draper, William H. *The Startup Game: Inside the Partnership Between Venture Capitalists and Entrepreneurs*. New York, NY: Palgrave Macmillan, 2011.

Dyer, Jeff, Hal Gregersen, and Clayton M. Christensen. *The Innovator's DNA: Mastering the 5 Skills of Disruptive Innovators*. Boston, MA: Harvard Business Press, 2011.

Eliot, Jay. *The Steve Jobs Way: iLeadership for a New Generation*. New York, NY: Vanguard Press, 2011.

Gegax, Tom, and Phil Bosta. *The Big Book of Small Business: You Don't Run Your Business by the Seat of Your Pants*. New York, NY: Harper Business, 2007.

Harris, Tom. *Start-up: A Practical Guide to Starting and Running a New Business*. New York, NY: Springer, 2010.

Hsieh, Tony. *Deliver Happiness: A Path to Profits, Passion, and Purpose*. New York, NY: Business Plus, 2010.

Isaacson, Walter. *Steve Jobs*. New York, NY: Simon & Schuster, 2011.

Jarvis, Jeff. *What Would Google Do?* New York, NY: HarperBusiness, 2009.

Kinsley, Michael, ed. *Creative Capitalism: A Conversation with Bill Gates, Warren Buffet, and Other Economic Leaders*. New York, NY: Simon & Schuster, 2009.

Lesinski, Jeanne M. *Bill Gates: Entrepreneur and Philanthropist*. Minneapolis, MN: Twenty-First Century Books, 2009.

Levy, Steven. *In the Plex.: How Google Thinks, Works, and Shapes Our Lives*. New York, NY: Simon & Schuster, 2011.

Livingston, Jessica. *Founders at Work: Stories of Startups' Early Days*. New York, NY: Apress, 2008.

Moritz, Michael. *Return to the Little Kingdom: Steve Jobs and the Creation of Apple*. New York, NY: Overlook Press, 2010.

Motley Fool, and Louann Lofton. *Warren Buffett Invests Like a Girl: And Why You Should, Too*. New York, NY: HarperBusiness, 2011.

Murphy, Bill, Jr. *The Intelligent Entrepreneur: How Three Harvard Business School Graduates Learned the 10 Rules of Successful Entrepreneurship*. New York, NY: Henry Holt and Co., 2010.

Rankin, Kenrya. *Start It Up: The Complete Teen Business Guide to Turning Your Passions into Pay*. Orlando, FL: Zest Books, 2011.

Ries, Eric. *The Lean Startup—How Today's Entrepreneurs Use Continuous Innovation to Create Radically Successful Businesses*. New York, NY: Crown Business, 2011.

Rogoff, Edward G. *Bankable Business Plans*. 2nd ed. Davis, CA: Rowhouse Publishing, 2007.

Schepp, Brad, and Debra Schepp. *Amazon Top Seller Secrets: Insider Tips from Amazon's Most Successful Sellers*. New York, NY: Amacom, 2009.

Schultz, Howard, and Joanne Gordon. *Onward: How Starbucks Fought for Its Life Without Losing Its Soul*. Emmaus, PA: Rodale Books, 2011.

Sims, Peter. *Little Bets: How Breakthrough Ideas Emerge from Small Discoveries*. New York, NY: Free Press, 2011.

Smith, Mari. *The New Relationship Marketing: How to Build a Large, Loyal, Profitable Network Using the Social Web*. Hoboken, NJ: Wiley, 2011.

Straus, Steven D. *The Small Business Bible: Everything You Need to Know to Succeed in Your Small Business*. 2nd ed. Hoboken, NJ: Wiley, 2008.

Warrillow, John. *Built to Sell: Creating a Business That Can Thrive Without You*. New York, NY: Portfolio/ Penguin, 2011.

Bibliography

Academy of Achievement. "Interview with Jeff Bezos."
    2001. Retrieved May 24, 2011 (http://www.achievement.
    org/autodoc/page/bez0int-1).

Bernhard, Kent, Jr. "Throwing a $250 Million
    Social Media Party." Portfolio.com, October 21,
    2010. Retrieved August 2, 2011 (http://www.
    portfolio.com/business-news/2010/10/21/
    kleiner-perkins-partners-with-facebook-amazon-
    and-zynga-on-social-app-fund).

Bezos Family Foundation. "Mission Statement" and
    "Students Rebuild." Retrieved July 7, 2011 (http://
    www.bezosfamilyfoundation.org).

Blue Origin, LLC. "Updates." January 2, 2007. Retrieved
    July 1, 2011 (http://www.blueorigin.com/letter.htm).

Brackett, Virginia. *Jeff Bezos*. New York, NY: Chelsea
    House Publishers, 2001.

Byers, Ann. *Jeff Bezos: The Founder of Amazon.com*. New
    York, NY: Rosen Publishing Group, 2007.

Chang, Kenneth. "NASA Awards $269 Million for Private
    Projects." *New York Times*, April 18, 2011. Retrieved
    July 15, 2011 (http://www.nytimes.com/2011/04/19/
    science/space/19nasa.html?_r=1).

Chang, Kenneth. "Rocket Financed by Amazon Founder
    Crashes in Test." *New York Times*, September 2,

2011. Retrieved September 4, 2011 (http://www.
nytimes.com/2011/09/03/science/space/03rocket.
html?scp=1&sq=Blue%20Origin&st=cse).

Fowler, Geoffrey A. "Amazon Says WikiLeaks Violated
Terms of Service." *Wall Street Journal*, December 3,
2010. Retrieved June 5, 2011 (http://online.wsj.com/
article/SB100014240527487033775045756513214027
63304.html).

Galante, Joseph, Olga Kharif, and Pavel Alpeyev. "Sony
Network Breach Shows Amazon Cloud's Appeal for
Hackers." *Bloomsburg Businessweek*, May 16, 2011.
Retrieved July 5, 2011 (http://www.businessweek.
com/news/2011-05-16/sony-network-breach-shows-
amazon-cloud-s-appeal-for-hackers.html).

Kang, Cecilia. "Amazon Takes Aim at Apple's iPad with
New $199 Kindle Fire Tablet." *Washington Post*,
September 28, 2011. Retrieved October 12, 2011
(http://www.washingtonpost.com/business/economy/
amazon-blazes-into-computing-with-new-fire-tablet/
2011/09/28/gIQAnQUl4K_story.html).

Landrum, Gene. *Entrepreneurial Genius: The Power
of Passion*. Burlington, ON: Brendan Kelly
Publishing, 2003.

Levy, Steven. "The Future of Reading." *Newsweek*, November
17, 2007. Retrieved July 1, 2011 (http://www.newsweek.
com/2007/11/17/the-future-of-reading.html).

Levy, Steven. "Playing with Fire: Amazon Launches $200 Tablet, Slashes Kindle Prices." *Wired*, September 28, 2011. Retrieved October 1, 2011 (http://www.wired.com/epicenter/2011/09/amazon).

Marcus, James. *Amazonia: Five Years at the Epicenter of Dot.com Juggernaut*. Rev. ed. New York, NY: New Press, 2004.

Milliot, Jim. "PW's Person of the Year: Jeff Bezos." *Publishers Weekly*, December 8, 2008. Retrieved June 7, 2011 (http://www.publishersweekly.com/pw/by-topic/authors/interviews/article/17160-pw--s-person-of-the-year-jeff-bezos-.html).

Patterson, Thom. "Can One Idea Be Energy's Holy Grail?" CNN.com, June 27, 2011. Retrieved July 8, 2011. (http://articles.cnn.com/2011-06-27/tech/fusion_1_hot-fusion-holy-grail-junk-mail?_s=PM:TECH).

Princeton University. "2010 Baccalaureate Remarks by Jeff Bezos." May 30, 2010. Retrieved July 17, 2011 (http:www.princeton.edu/main/news/archive/S27/52/51O99/index.xml).

Ramo, Joshua Cooper. "Jeffrey Preston Bezos: 1999 Person of the Year." *Time*, December 27, 1999. Retrieved May 25, 2011 (http://www.time.com/time/magazine/article/0,9171,992927,00.html).

Reynolds, Paul. "Will Amazon Make a Tablet? 'Stay Tuned," Says Jeff Bezos." ConsumerReports.org,

May 11, 2011. Retrieved June 15, 2011 (http://news.consumerreports.org/electronics/2011/05/will-amazon-make-a-tablet-stay-tuned-says-jeff-bezos.html).

Robinson, Tom. *Jeff Bezos: Amazon.com Architect*. Edina, MN: ABDO Publishing Company, 2010.

Ryan, Bernard, Jr. *Jeff Bezos: Business Executive and Founder of Amazon.com*. New York, NY: Ferguson Publishing Company, 2005.

Spector, Robert. *Amazon.com: Get Big Fast*. New York, NY: Harper Paperbacks, 2002.

Stone, Brad. "Amazon Erases Orwell Books from Kindle." *New York Times*, July 18, 2009. Retrieved June 21, 2011 (http://www.nytimes.com/2009/07/18/technology/companies/18amazon.html?scp=1&sq=Amazon%20erases%20orwell%20books%20from%20Kindle&st=cse).

Streitfeld, David. "Amazon's Profit Falls, but Beats Expectations, as Company Invests." *New York Times*, July 26, 2011. Retrieved July 27, 2011 (http://www.nytimes.com/2011/07/27/technology/amazons-earnings-beat-expectations-even-as-profits-fall.html?_r=1&scp=1&sq=Amazons%20profit%20falls%20&st=cse).

Streitfeld, David. "California Lawmakers Give Amazon Tax Reprieve." *New York Times*, September 10, 2011.

Retrieved September 12, 2011 (http://www.nytimes.
com/2011/09/11/technology/california-votes-to-give-
amazon-a-sales-tax-reprieve.html).

Wortham, Jenna, and David Streitfeld. "Amazon's Tablet
Leads to Its Store." *New York Times*, September 28,
2011. Retrieved September 29, 2011 (http://www.
nytimes.com/2011/09/29/technology/amazon-unveils-
tablet-that-undercuts-ipads-price.html?pagewanted=
2&_r=1&sq=amazon%20tablet%20leads%20to%20
its%20store&st=cse&scp=1).

Index

ABOUT THE AUTHOR

Jennifer Landau received her MA in creative writing from New York University and her MST in general and special education from Fordham University. An experienced editor, she has also published both fiction and nonfiction, including *The Right Words: Knowing What to Say and How to Say It*. In addition to her work as a special education teacher, Landau has taught writing to high school students and senior citizens.

She has a particular interest in expanding inclusion opportunities for special education students and teaching these students self-advocacy skills. A longtime Amazon customer and Kindle user, Landau is fascinated by the way technology has changed the face of publishing for both readers and writers. When she is not writing, she enjoys reading and spending time outdoors with her young son.

PHOTO CREDITS